Sleeping With Your Eyes Open
WARNING DREAMS

Sleeping With Your Eyes Open

WARNING DREAMS

By Craig Groethe

**What you need to know
and how to respond**

● **RANSOM PUBLISHING**

**Third Printing
January 2011**

• RANSOM PUBLISHING

Unless otherwise noted, Bible quotations are taken from the New King James Version.

The Interpreters
801 13 Avenue South
St. Cloud, MN 56301

Designed by Allan H. Johnson
www.AllanHJohnson.com

ISBN: 978-1-61658-030-8

Acknowledgements

I want to especially thank Kate Minion for her expertise in helping me doing the final proofing. This book wouldn't be possible without all those who have given me permission to include their dreams and testimonies. Thank you for your contributions. I want to thank all those who encouraged me through the long process of getting the book done. I am grateful for those who helped with finances in order for me to do my writing and get the book to press. Thank you all from the bottom of my heart.

CONTENTS

This book is dedicated to my wife and
best friend, Vicky. It is through her grace
and unconditional love for me, in spite
of my unworthiness, that I have most
clearly heard God tell me that
He loves me.

INTRODUCTION

In the exploration of dreams scientists have discovered that a human has between three to seven dreams each night. When a person says he/she doesn't dream, it is simply that they generally don't remember their dreams.

I have listened to over 5,000 dreams the last ten years for the purpose of interpreting them. I have journaled my own personal dreams during that same time. I have witnessed first hand, dreams that foretold future events in my personal life or in the lives of my loved ones. I came to know these as prophetic warning dreams. As I would speak about my personal experience in public teaching or speaking engagements, people would always approach me afterwards and explain that they had similar warning dreams, foretelling the death of a close loved one. This became very common, and I began recording their stories and experiences as I heard them.

Certainly, dreams that come from beyond are not limited to just bring warning. Dreams can bring encouragement, instruction, revelation, direction, comfort, enlightenment, and much more that can make our lives much richer. However, very little is known about warning dreams. It is critical that we come understand warning dreams as the very health and lives of people and loved ones are at stake if we do not.

I believe there is a Giver of dreams that is outside of our self. It may be defined as an Energy Force, God, or Creator. Most commonly we use the term God. I have observed that this force, which I will simply call God, brings us revelation of the future out of love, care, or protection. Unfortunately, we are ill prepared to deal with these warnings, and they have thus been misunderstood and misinterpreted by most.

I have further observed that this God loves everyone. People have experienced this phenomenon regardless of faith or lack thereof. Whether one is Jewish, Islamic, Christian, or of any other belief, they all are recipients of this God's love and protection through His warnings. Therefore I encourage people of any and every faith to read this book. I hope this book will bring relief, re-solve, and understanding for what people have experienced or what they may one day experience.

Though I personally introduce myself to people as a follower of God through Christ Jesus, I come short of calling myself Christian, at times, only because I know there are Christians who believe in Christ but don't necessarily follow Him. While this book will be informative to everyone regardless of their belief, I have directed it to the Christian audience for the purpose of convincing those of my belief that this is a reality that is a Biblical and historical reality that exists today and is valid for every believer in Christ. I have used the Scriptures to validate my claims in my attempt to convince and persuade the Christian community of the vital need to adopt these doctrines into their belief system. Indeed Christians have been lag-ging way behind in understanding these mysteries. It is my hope and prayer that I will bring truth and revelation to all those who have ears to hear. My desire is that prophetic warning dreams will one day be accepted by most as a natural and common occurrence in peoples lives everywhere. With knowledge of how to respond to warning dreams I hope to help make these types of dreams a common preventative medicine that is usable to all.

You will notice a repetitive theme as you read this book. We need to believe this Loving Force speaks to mankind through dreams. We need to pay attention to Him and to these dreams. We need to learn to interpret these dreams as accurately as possible. We need to respond appropriately and faithfully to these warnings in order to walk through this under the protection and guidance of this loving One who is constantly watching over His Creation.

Craig Groethe
The Interpreters
October 9th, 2009

CHAPTER 1

THE BEGINNING OF MY DREAM EXPERIENCE

The Prophesy

I received a prophesy in 1998 stating, in part, that I would "see dreams and visions", I have been pressing into and seeking the Lord in this area that is little accepted or understood by the present day church. While I always have dreamed and have recognized some of my dreams as being very significant, I never have paid that much attention to them in general. I did not realize how powerfully these dreams could speak to my life. More importantly, I didn't know how to respond to these dreams.

This prophecy led me to begin journaling my dreams. In this

simple attempt to be faithful to the prophetic word given over me, I diligently wrote down the dreams I had and meditated on them. I reviewed them often, asking God what was to be revealed through them. Up until that time, serving the Lord for 25 years, I had never heard a single teaching on the significance of dreams or visions in present day Christianity. I never came across a book on the subject. I didn't know which dreams were from God, or indeed if any were from God.

As I continued journaling over the next three years, I sought the Lord for understanding and interpretation. I still hadn't heard of any teaching or books on the subject. The Christian bookstores had nothing. If there were something out there that was biblically based, I was not aware of it. Certainly to venture too far into this arena may be viewed, in my circles, as too much like New Age, the occult, or the like. I hung onto Christ's words in John 16:13 saying that the Spirit would guide us into all truth. I resolved to depend upon the Holy Spirit alone to lead me into the truth concerning dreams. The training began.

As the first few months passed, I sensed certain dreams were urging me to active participation in them. After roughly fifty dreams and six months of journaling, I found myself participating, mostly through prayer. Some seemed to speak to me urging a response and action on my part. I began practicing in this manner. At times, when I had a dream including another friend or acquaintance, I would call that person. I would ask them if anything was going on in their lives that may parallel my dream. More often than not, the dream would indeed be a reflection of something significant in their lives. I would make note of that. As I continued to grow in this area of understanding, I was "off" in my interpretations more than "on". But I kept at it, for the most part, privately listening and pondering my own personal dreams. Soon I began sharing with my close Christian friends some of the significant things I had found in my dreams.

As time passed, I realized that it wasn't simply coincidence that certain things occurring in my life were reflected through my dreams. My wife and I began bringing up the subject of dreams when we would meet with friends. Dreams became the main topic of conversation amongst us, and we met more and more often. The revelations that poured forth into this small group were amazing. We talked about the dreams we were having, ranging from the craziest and zaniest to the seemingly mundane. Within a year, I realized that a new world of dreams and visions was springing up before our lives; fruit coming forth in the study of these dreams. Once in a while, profound interpretation would come forth and would transform us. We began taking these dreams more seriously. We took direction, instruction, revelation and encouragement from them. We made adjustments in our lives according to the convictions God was attempting to communicate to us. Then, one by one, people began contacting me with their dreams. I would listen carefully, giving the dreamer anything I felt the Holy Spirit was saying in the way of interpretation, making sure the person understood that I was only a babe in this and a learning student. Surprisingly, many people responded such that God was truly breaking through into their lives.

Finally, after interpreting around two hundred dreams for others, not including my own, I found a couple of books from Catholic authors who had written on dreams. Shortly after that I was told of a man named John Paul Jackson who taught a course on the subject. I grabbed the first plane I could and went to one of his classes. I sat listening to him teach on many of the same things the Holy Spirit had revealed to me. It was a great confirmation to me. Over the next few years, more and more books were popping up from Christian authors who had similarly come to learn how to interpret dreams through the power and inspiration of the Holy Spirit. Many Christian bookstores would not sell them. Books on the subject started popping up at various Christian prophetic conferences I attended. I also searched and purchased a few books on the Internet regarding Biblical dream interpretation. These books confirmed that I was on the right track in the things I learned about the interpretation of dreams and well as visions. They were great encouragement to me in continuing on this journey.

Seven Days & Nights in the Fruit Cellar

There was more to that early prophesy given over me in 1998. The leading of the Lord, through the prophetic word, also brought me to a weeklong retreat in January of 2000. I went to a summerhouse on the edge of a tiny community in North Dakota. The prophecy stated I would spend some "time alone with Him without interruption" in order for Him to "tell me some things and show me some things". I decided to take this winter retreat of silence and solitude. I was surprised that just a couple weeks short of leaving for this retreat, the Lord showed me that my time was to include spending time in the basement's fruit cellar, and in the dark as well. Being faithful to His leading, on a cold Thursday winter evening, my brother Kent drove me into North Dakota. He left me alone at this heated house, and the seven-day journey began.

It was during that stay that the Lord certainly did show and tell me some things. I tell people that if you say that you don't hear from God, "Try seven days and nights in a fruit cellar. You will hear from God!" During that seven-day period, the Lord gave me some dreams that certainly had significance, not only for my life, but also for the lives of others. I must say, those seven days had the most profound impact on my life.

Ready to Minister in Pierre, SD

About two months prior to going down into the fruit cellar, I called a business client of mine who is the Recorder of Deeds at a courthouse about 30 miles from Pierre, South Dakota. I had a small business performing record preservation work in county courthouses. My client and I shared regarding our mutual faith in Christ as well. She mentioned that she had recently joined an Aglow group in Pierre. Aglow is an international women's ministry meeting in various communities around the United States and many countries in the world. Upon telling her about the dreams I had been interpreting for others, she suggested I come out and speak at one of their Aglow meetings. My immediate thought was, "I really have nothing to say to a group of women in Pierre, South Dakota!" I quickly changed the subject and shortly after, our conversation ended.

Soon after I returned home from my seven-day retreat, I had a dream concerning this Recorder. In the dream, this county Recorder was in my van with me as I pulled up to the curb in downtown Pierre. I have never been to Pierre, South Dakota in real life. I turned to her and stated that I was now ready to come and speak at her Aglow group meeting. There were two more scenes to the dream. When I woke up in the morning, I faithfully wrote down the dream and felt compelled to respond by calling this Recorder. This was on a Saturday morning. I was so moved by the dream that I dialed directory service for that community, got her home phone number, called her, and left a message saying, reluctantly but obediently, that I was now ready to come to Pierre and speak at her women's group. It seemed to me that I was to speak concerning this very dream. I knew this dream was about them, even though I had absolutely no idea what the dream meant at the time. Now it was simply in the Lord's hands whether or not I would be invited to speak. Honestly, I was hoping that I would not end up being invited. But, lo and behold, about five days later, I received a phone call from a woman named Karon Young, the president of the local chapter of Aglow in Pierre. She was following up to a phone call from the Recorder. I explained that I had a dream revealinng I was ready to speak at their meeting. I was to speak concerning the interpretation of the dream, as I believed it was the very word from the Lord for their local Aglow chapter. She said that she believed that my dream was from God. The date was set for me to come speak in August, which was approximately four months away. I spent hours and hours over those next four months, praying for the interpretation and seeking the meaning of the dream with its three scenes. The Lord was faithful to give me much revelation concerning it.

My wife, Vicky, and I drove to Pierre in August on a Saturday afternoon. I presented a three-hour presentation interpretation of the dream to about twenty women and their spouses gathered in a home. My presentation included overhead projections of each scene with many details. In the end, the group affirmed that this dream was truly sent from God. The Lord confirmed the event with powerful signs and wonders that occurred in that home. Thus, my ministry of dreams began in earnest.

CHAPTER 2

MY FIRST
WARNING DREAM

I had been interpreting and recording my dreams for only a short while when I received what I discerned to be my first warning dream from the Lord.

The Head On Collision Dream

I dreamed Vicky, my wife, and I were driving down a four-lane highway. I'm confused as to whether it was four-lanes or two-lanes. The car ahead of us turned into the lane of oncoming traffic. We witnessed the car slamming head on into an oncoming car. We missed being part of the accident by a small margin as we swerved over into the lane to the right. As we passed the head on collision, we saw the destruction. I realized that everyone in both vehicles had to have died.

I woke up from this dream on a Saturday morning, went into the living room, and sat down on a loveseat to write down the dream. When I journaled, "I was driving down a four-lane," I was confused as to whether or not it was a two-lane or a four-lane. You know how obscure dreams are; sometimes you just can't explain completely, or you just don't know something for sure. You know, but you can't put it into words. I resolved to write that it was a four lane. I finished journaling the dream, put the journal down and asked the Lord for an interpretation. As I pondered the dream, I looked at it symbolically, which I believe most dreams are. It just didn't seem to make any sense. I then asked the Lord, "Are you telling me this is a literal car accident of Satan's devising that has yet to occur?" I felt an immediate nod in the affirmative, "Yes!" from the Spirit. I responded by praying out loud, in essence, "Okay then, in the name of Jesus, I break off this assignment of the enemy to cause that head on accident". I finished with an Amen, and went about my day.

The Dream Made Manifest

That evening, my oldest son, Carey, who was, in a Christian band at the time, was playing in a "battle of the bands" in a community 60 miles away. The winner of this night's contest would be invited to play at "Sonshine," an annual well known Outdoor Christian Music Festival occurring in Willmar, Minnesota each summer.

The same evening, my wife and I were over at friends. At around 10:00 p.m. I received a call from my son announcing his band just won first place. This meant they would play at the summer festival. I rejoiced with him and asked what time he might be home. Since he would not be back until after midnight, I told him I would see him in four or five days as I had to leave early in the morning to drive to Missouri on a business trip.

The next morning I picked up my sister. We were heading

down the highway to Missouri when Pam said, "Hey, neat thing about the kids doing so well at the concert last night. Did you hear about the near car accident?" I responded, "No! What near car accident?" She said, "The near car accident that Carey and the band were involved in."

She told me that on the drive home from the concert around 1:00 in the morning, her daughter Emily, along with friends in her car, were following directly behind the band on a state highway. Suddenly the band's SUV with Carey driving pulled into the opposite lane attempting to pass the vehicle ahead of him. There were three other cars coming in close proximity from the opposite direction, all at speeds of about sixty miles per hour. Emily and the other passenger in the front seat immediately began screaming and broke into tears at the fearful expectation of a crash. They watched the vehicle being passed quickly veer to the shoulder of the road, as did each of the oncoming vehicles from their respective lanes. Carey, at the last minute, swerved the vehicle and trailer back into his lane, and missed a head on collision with the first car by a small margin. Pam said that Emily woke her up when she got home and shared the horrifying story.

Upon hearing the story, I was quite upset. As I continued to think about it for the next hour, my dream came to mind. I blurted out, "Pam! Grab my dream journal in the back seat!" She found the dream for me and read it back. We both were startled and amazed that it was incredibly close to that which actually occurred. Pam told me the story from her daughter's point of view, the same point of view I had in *my* dream of following the vehicle. Certainly this had to be the work of God giving warning through a dream! Had my response of praying saved the lives of my son and all the others? Over the next few days I thought of how critical it was for me to write that dream down, taking the simple action step of praying. I came to believe Satan had intended to take the life of my son and others. He failed, apparently by my intercession. I wondered if other people had been prompted by the Lord and faithfully interceded concerning this near car accident.

Upon returning from my trip, I asked my son what on earth he was thinking to pass a vehicle, on a highway, in the middle of the night, pulling a large trailer none-the-less, with cars coming full speed in the opposite direction, when he obviously was too close to be able to pass successfully. He responded, "Dad, I was confused. I thought I was on a *four-lane*!" Instantly, I remembered how I also was confused in writing my dream as to whether I was in a four-lane or a two-lane!

> *Hosea 4:6 My people are destroyed for lack of knowledge. Because you have rejected knowledge, I also will reject you from being priest for Me; Because you have forgotten the law of your God, I also will forget your children.*

That's Why Many People Die Prematurely

Later that day I also learned that my daughter, Christine, and my other son, Paul, were also in that Sport Utility Vehicle with the band. Satan's assignment was to take out every child of mine that night, as well as the other band members. My dream didn't reveal who it was in those vehicles! What if I would have ignored the dream and not prayed? I was afraid to think of what might have happened. Days later the Lord spoke to my heart and said, "That's why many people die prematurely and continue to die." We aren't paying attention to God's warnings. He is doing His part in giving the warnings. We must do ours by hearing these warnings. We must learn how to interpret these mysteries, be faithful in responding to them, and understand *how* to respond appropriately so that lives aren't cut short.

God's Work Continues

In the months that followed, my son's band played not only at Sonshine, but in many other venues. This included going on a national tour with Acquire the Fire Ministries. They played for up to 12,000 youth at a time in major cities and venues throughout the country. The band was approached by two high school principals in our community to perform worship music once a week. The band had a profound impact on these schools proclaiming Christ in song and worship as the music penetrated out into the hallways throughout much of the school buildings in that hour each week, for two consecutive years. Among other high school performances, they were asked by their senior class to do the special music at their class graduation ceremony. Satan obviously had other plans, but the love of God kept him from completing his assignment.

People attending my dream classes and people elsewhere have shared with me that although they don't write down their dreams, they always remember the "God" dreams. Those are the dreams they say they will never forget, certainly not within hours after they wake up from the dream. I respond with this dream that was to have taken the lives of all my children and others. I tell them that this car accident dream was *not* one in which I woke up shaken and emotionally disturbed to any degree. I go on to say that, if I had not written it down as soon as I did, after I woke up, I would have forgotten the dream by noon. This emphasizes the extreme importance of writing dreams down as soon as possible after waking from sleep. It illustrates the need to interpret the dreams correctly and respond faithfully and timely to how the Holy Spirit would unction us to respond.

Drowning in Lake Superior

There is one other note regarding this warning dream. A couple years later, I was in Duluth, Minnesota teaching a two-day class on dreams. I had just finished teaching the attendees about warning dreams and had told the "Head On Collision" warning dream. When I finished, I announced we would take a ten-minute break. A small woman immediately walked up to me, thanking me for telling that story. She then said it ministered so much to her because three months earlier she had received a dream in which her son drowned in Lake Superior. There was a pause, and I said in a very soft pitch, "Well...*did* he?" to which she responded, "Yes! He drowned in Lake Superior two weeks later." She continued, "I didn't know I was supposed to pray, Craig!" I gently but firmly responded by saying, "I am so sorry, but this is *not* your fault. We were never taught about this. The church as a whole does not know how to identify and respond to these warnings." I was able to again emphasize what loving God we have who gives us warning when our loved ones are in danger. We must learn this language of dreams in which the Lord pours out His love and protection for us."

CHAPTER 3

SEPTEMBER 11ᵀᴴ WARNINGS

The next discernable warning dreams also came very early in my learning. They came in the way of one dream, one vision, and a dream my oldest son, Carey, had. He was nineteen years old at the time. These three instances were warnings leading up to the September eleventh terrorist attacks on America in 2001.

Urgent Banging on the Door Dream

August 23, 2001

At 5:30 a.m. this morning I was awakened by a loud and frantic banging on our back-porch door! As soon as it started, I heard our dog, Pepper, barking in response to this pounding. It startled me, and I instantly sat up in bed and lunged over my wife's body. I was trying to look out the back window and open it to inquire who was out there. As I did so, I was frantically asking Vicky who it might be and what might be going on at this time of the morning. Vicky didn't respond, and to my surprise, I turned to find that she was still sleeping. How could she be still sleeping when the banging virtually shook the whole house. Most of our neighbors had to awakened from such a clamor? Then, I realized the knocking had stopped as well as the dog's barking. I continued looking out the window from on the bed to see if anyone might be leaving the porch. I waited for a minute and then realized that there wasn't anyone at the back door at all. I finally surmised I had apparently been dreaming. But the jolt the event produced to my system with all the panic knocks gave me a feeling of urgency. Something was terribly wrong, and I was being warned about it. It was like each knock signaled an "emergency" like 9-1-1. It seemed to carry with it a sense that something very big was wrong. That it was global or something much larger than just my family. With the knowledge of this, I immediately got out of bed, ran into the living room, knelt down in front of the couch and interceded on behalf of that intrusion. I prayed for what seemed to be an hour or so before I felt the release to go back to bed.

The Headless Horseman Warning Vision

September 3rd, 2001

As I lay in bed at 11:30 p.m. on September 3, 2001, I had a snapshot type vision of a headless horseman riding on a galloping gray roan horse. It was coming towards me down a road. The skies were very dark and gray. I was close up as I watched. When the quick vision ended, it left me with a very eerie feeling. I couldn't shake it, and I didn't know how to respond to it.

My Son Carey's 9-11 Missile Dream

September 6, 2001, 5:45 a.m.

I was with a group of kids from my church. We were outside watching the stars. There was what looked like a shooting star. Everyone turned to look as it got farther across the sky. We realized it was not a shooting star, but a missile. Suddenly, another missile shot into the air from the horizon and blew up the first one. It was obvious we were under attack. I learned that America was under attack by Iraq. Then, we were sitting on the lawn of (St. Cloud) Tech High School. Another missile came into the atmosphere and disappeared into the horizon. A "bang" was heard, and the ground shook! Outside lights went out and on again twice. We knew we had better go in and take cover inside a nearby Assembly of God Church. We went to the basement, where, I recall saying it was safer. There were a few events that went on down there. A small missile landed in one room just as my family walked in. I took off out of there yelling to Paul, my brother, to run. It blew up, but no one was hurt. Then, in another room, a group or committee of people, were meeting discussing action that needed to be taken. I had a bad feeling about those people. It was like they were trying to take over something. These, by the way, were old church people. The basement started to fill with more people. Mom and I were worried that we would somehow lose our spot inside. We took a list with our names on it and hung it up downstairs. In the course of all this [his dream goes on with more scenes]…I was explaining the dream to my dad, when I woke up.

Interpreting the Warnings

On September 11 of 2001, when the tragedies happened, I was on a business trip in St. Joseph, Missouri. Upon hearing of the attacks I quickly finished a meeting I was in and decided to head back home to Minnesota to be with my family. Driving home, my son Carey called to ask if I had heard about the attacks. He called me back moments later and said, "Dad! My Missile Dream!"

In the process of learning about dreams, these were the first dreams along with the "Head-on Collision Dream," I recognized to be warnings from the Lord. Even though the "Urgent Banging Door" dream, was nineteen days prior to the actual event, I quickly associated it with the tragedies of September 11th. How? First of all, the emotions I felt on September 11th were the same I felt in my dream. In addition, I knew intuitively that both my dream and vision were speaking about something big, something possibly global. Sometimes, you just will have a knowing that comes with a dream. I learned that the emotions in the dream, as well as the emotions you feel upon waking from a dream could have just as much to do with the dream as the dream itself. The same goes for what I call "knowings". There will be times in a dream that, beyond what is observed or experienced you "know" things concerning the dream. You have a specific or general knowledge in the dream.

Furthermore, the first dream gave me a message, one of urgency and of emergency—"Call 9-1-1"! When it was first said that the attacks "coincidently" happened on the date of 9/11, I was further strengthened in my belief that my "Banging on the Door Dream" was a warning of the events that took place on 9/11.

Concerning the Headless Horseman Vision, I was less moved emotionally. I wasn't sure what it meant until I heard President Bush respond to the terrorist attacks. He said the tragedy was committed by "A faceless coward". I instantly was reminded of the vision as I put "The Headless Horseman" and "a faceless coward" together as being parallel to one another.

Carey's Missile Dream was incredible! There was so much that matched what took place on 9/11. He told me later, when he was observing the first missile, he was facing east from the perspective of living in Minnesota. He was facing New York City. He said that the first missile was almost at the horizon when another missile shot into the air and blew up the first one. What he saw in the dream was really two planes exploding on the same city block seventeen minutes apart from one another. In addition, someone spoke of the planes being used as "missiles" in the attacks. Interestingly, Carey had knowledge in the dream that "America was under attack by Iraq". The war in Iraq didn't begin until March of 2003. At the time of the attack on America, we were not in conflict with Iraq to the heightened point that Carey was conscious of. With the third missile, "a 'bang' was heard and the ground shook"! Certainly there was a loud explosion and shaking of the ground as that third plane piled into the Pentagon. And last of all, the fourth missile, in which Carey said that, "no one was hurt". No one was hurt, "outside of the plane", due to the heroic efforts of the men and women on Flight 93. In addition, they had a "list with our names on it and hung up" as did those who, searching for lost loved ones, hung up flyers with pictures and descriptions on store windows near the site of the Twin Towers. Amazing!

Responding to the Warnings

So, how did I know what to do when receiving this dream and vision? I didn't know exactly. The dream beckoned me for a response to answer the door, to "answer the call" so to speak. It was a messenger with a message of: "We need help", or "call 9-1-1"! "There is something BIG brewing in the atmosphere". Will you help? Will you pray? Will you respond? Because it came to me through a dream and later through a vision, I knew I had to be faithful and obedient. I had promised God that I would heed the prophesy He had given me in 1998. I would pay attention to these things He shows me. I owed Him my faithfulness, and my obedience to His promptings.

In the case of "The Headless Horseman", when I received the vision, I did not respond by praying. I hadn't been moved emotionally by the vision even though it was dark and eerie. I have now learned that I should have responded to those signs as well as others. When Carey woke, being overcome by the emotions of the dream as well as being shaken by the scenes in the dream, he felt the need to pray. He got out of bed, and on his knees at the bedside, interceded on behalf of the dream for a lengthy period of time. We don't remember now if I had previously shared my two journaled warnings with him or not. He simply responded in the way that seemed natural to him and was faithful to what the Lord had shown him. He was also terrified and shaken at the events in the dream.

So why didn't our prayers stop the 9/11 tragedy? The scriptures say that we only "know in part". Sometimes, especially with larger events like what happened on September 11th, cancelling the assignment of an event this large takes more than just a few people hearing from heaven. I know that there are many other stories of people that *did* hear from God by various means, and respond by praying. Some had dreams, some had visions, and still others unctioning like that "pit in the stomach" feeling and knew enough to respond by interceding. In these cases we are each called on to do our part. Many did their part. We weren't able to cancel the assignment of the enemy totally in this, but we did help minimize what could and should have been a much worse tragedy. We have since read and heard it said that there should have been many more people in the Towers at that time of day. We have since heard and read stories of many who called in sick or took the day off at the last moment. Some were detoured and delayed in arriving at work. Many more should have died in those towers that day. I do not believe that these were all coincidences. Unseen powers were at work in response to the intercession of those hearing the prophetic warnings and interceding.

Looking back, do you remember receiving any warning from heaven leading up to September 11th? I am not suggesting everyone is called to hear every warning from heaven. But we are each called to do our part. The more faithful we each are, the more, I believe, we will see life and life "more abundantly" spring forth in our lives and the lives of others.

CHAPTER 4

WARNING DREAMS IN THE BIBLE

My attention and searching concerning God's warnings was heightened by the events and testimonies of my family's warning dreams and by the woman's loss of her son. I took a deeper look into the Scriptures, reading about God's warnings to man in both the Old and New Testament.

Abimelech

> _Genesis 20:1 And Abraham journeyed from there to the South, and dwelt between Kadesh and Shur, and stayed in Gerar. 2 Now Abraham said of Sarah his wife, "She is my_

*sister." And **Abimelech king of Gerar** sent and took Sarah. 3 But **God came to Abimelech in a dream by night**, and said to him, "Indeed you are a dead man because of the woman whom you have taken, for she is a man's wife." 4 But Abimelech had not come near her; and he said, "Lord, will You slay a righteous nation also? 5 "Did he not say to me, 'She is my sister'? And she, even she herself said, 'He is my brother.' In the integrity of my heart and innocence of my hands I have done this." 6 And **God said to him in a dream**, "Yes, I know that you did this in the integrity of your heart. For I also withheld you from sinning against Me; therefore I did not let you touch her. 7 "Now therefore, restore the man's wife; for he is a prophet, and he will pray for you and you shall live. But if you do not restore her, know that you shall surely die, you and all who are yours."*

It's interesting to note that God gives a warning through a dream to a pagan king. Through this dream alone: God comes to Abimelech. God speaks to him revealing the knowledge of the truth of his situation. Abimelech responds; acknowledging and addressing Him as Lord and making his defense in response. God warns and gives instruction to Abimelech; he and his family would die if he didn't restore Sarah to Abraham. Interestingly, Abimelech goes to Abraham and gives Abraham what would amount to a word of knowledge, telling him that Sarah was his wife and revealing to Abraham his secret plan. The story ends with Abimelech acknowledging this warning dream and avoiding death by restoring Sarah to Abraham as well as giving Abraham sheep, oxen, and servants. Abraham indeed prayed for healing over Abimelech and his household. God did heal his family as all the wombs of the house of Abimelech had been closed up until that time. God gives a dream to a man who was not an apparent follower of Jehovah God. Abimelech, in turn, obeys just as the Lord commanded and was rewarded for that. What love God has for His Creation! Abimelech was wise enough to fear the Lord and obey what the Lord commanded in the dream.

Warning to the Magi in Bethlehem

Matthew 2:1 Now after Jesus was born in Bethlehem of Judea in the days of Herod the king, behold, **wise men** *from the East came to Jerusalem, 2 saying, "Where is He who has been born King of the Jews? For we have seen His star in the East and have come to worship Him." 3 When Herod the king heard this, he was troubled, and all Jerusalem with him. 4 And when he had gathered all the chief priests and scribes of the people together, he inquired of them where the Christ was to be born. 5 So they said to him, "In Bethlehem of Judea, for thus it is written by the prophet: 6 'But you, Bethlehem, in the land of Judah, Are not the least among the rulers of Judah; For out of you shall come a Ruler Who will shepherd My people Israel.'" 7 Then Herod, when he had secretly called the wise men, determined from them what time the star appeared. 8 And he sent them to Bethlehem and said, "Go and search carefully for the young Child, and when you have found Him, bring back word to me, that I may come and worship Him also." 9 When they heard the king, they departed; and behold, the star which they had seen in the East went before them, till it came and stood over where the young Child was. 10 When they saw the star, they rejoiced with exceedingly great joy. 11 And when they had come into the house, they saw the young Child with Mary His mother, and fell down and worshiped Him. And when they had opened their treasures, they presented gifts to Him: gold, frankincense, and myrrh. 12 Then,* **being divinely warned in a dream that they should not return to Herod, they departed for their own country another way.**

The Greek word used for "wise" men is "magi". Magi were pagan sorcerers, magicians or astrologers. They probably came from Persian Arabia and were apparently aware of the Jewish prophecies concerning the coming Jewish Messiah.

After a stop in Jerusalem and receiving instructions from King Herod to bring back word of the Messiah's whereabouts, they continued being led by the star to the manger in Bethlehem. They worshipped Jesus. I find it amazing that the only other account of visitors to the manger in Bethlehem were a few shepherds. They were living nearby and were told of the baby Jesus by a band of angels that showed up in the field where they were tending their sheep? My question is: Where were all the Jews, God's chosen people? As prophesied, here is the Messiah and Savior in Bethlehem, and the only ones who show up are a few shepherds and what we would call today, unsaved psychics? Reluctantly, I am resigned to say here, "Well done faithful magicians!"

So, where were the real believers? Where were the Jews? Amos may shed some light to this question.

> *Amos 8:11* *"Behold, the days are coming," says the Lord GOD, "That I will send a famine on the land, Not a famine of bread, Nor a thirst for water, But of hearing the words of the LORD.*

It was no secret that the Jew's hearts had grown hardened over time. The author of Hebrews tells us that the Jews had become hardened in their hearts to such a degree that they couldn't hear the voice of the Lord. They were filled with unbelief and disobedience. Amos does NOT say that there was a famine in the land "of the words of the Lord", but instead "of *hearing* the words of the Lord". We know about the four hundred years of silence when there was not a "word of the Lord" in the land up until John the Baptist. It wasn't because God wasn't speaking. God never stops speaking. God's chosen people stopped hearing. They had uncircumcised ears, eyes, and hearts. But before we get too hard on the Jews of that time, let's take a look at ourselves, and observe the modern day Christians in the Church of America.

I fear we too have grown hard of hearing. This in turn has produced unbelief and disobedience toward God in our own lives. Unbelief is a result of not being able to hear the Lord's voice. It is a result of rebelling and refusing to believe that which we do hear or have heard. It is a lack of paying attention to the things that God is saying and ignoring the means He uses to speak to us. It's no wonder that the Magi heard and responded. They were paying attention. Modern day psychics are not too different. For instance, why is it that they are the ones finding the missing persons over the years? They are greatly used and sought by police forces in many cities for help in solving crimes. Shouldn't it be Christians who should be finding the missing? Isn't that which is in us greater than that which is in the world? Look at what gifting Daniel and his three roommates possessed in Babylon

> _Daniel 1:20 And in all matters of wisdom and understanding about which the king examined them, he found them [Daniel, Hananiah, Mishael, and Azariah] ten times better than all the magicians and astrologers who were in all his realm._

And what about psychics prophesying of future events? Sometimes they get that right too! I thought that the devil doesn't know the future. That's the word I heard from many Christian scholars and teachers. I believe that Satan does not know the future. But then how do they know all these things? Here is my answer to these questions.

How Come Psychics are Stealing the Show?

Psychics and the like listen to unseen voices. They have ears to hear much in the supernatural world. In listening to the voices in the unseen atmosphere they do hear God's voice occasionally. They aren't stealing anything. That doesn't make them Christian, by any means. But God's voice is there to be heard. Abimelech heard it. The Magi heard from God and so did many more in the Bible who were not followers of Jehovah God. God does not discriminate when he shouts to earth from heaven. He created and loves everybody. In my opinion, the problem is that psychics listen to many voices not knowing or discerning the voices they hear. They are prone to follow strangers.

> *John 10: 4 "And when he (the Good Shepherd, Jesus)*
> *brings out his own sheep, he goes before them; and the sheep*
> *follow him, for they know his voice. 5 "Yet they will by no*
> *means follow a stranger, but will flee from him, for they do*
> *not know the voice of strangers."*

Those that are Christ's know his voice and do not listen to the voice of strangers. That is clear from the Parable of the Good Shepherd. We have the ability to discern through the Holy Spirit. However, that doesn't make Christians exempt from hearing other voices. Hearing comes through a proper condition of the heart. The Parable of the Sower calls it "good soil". Unfortunately we are not all in that good soil, having our ears and hearts circumcised. It is critical that we repent of this heart condition, as it exists in our lives, and come into greater and greater hearing of the voice of our Lord. He is always speaking. I tell people wherever I teach that I hear to such a small degree compared to the level God has called us to hear. I have repented. I have asked the Lord, and continue to ask Him, to open my ears and eyes to that which He is saying. Paying attention is key to starting this process. Years later, after my turning and paying attention, I hear to such a greater degree than when I first began recording my dreams. What I have heard has changed my life, the life of my family, and the life of others in a tremendously radical way!

Christians are often heard asking, "How do we know if it is God, the devil, or our own self speaking to us?" We need to develop a discipline of paying attention. We need to learn the language of God, the means he uses to direct His thoughts and His ways to us as believers. This language that God uses to speak to us is in no way limited to the written Word of the Scriptures.

> *Mark 4:10 But when He was alone, those around Him*
> *with the twelve asked Him about the parable [of the*
> *sower].... 11 And He said to them, "To you it has been*
> *given to know the mystery of the kingdom of God; ...22*
> *"For there is nothing hidden which will not be revealed,*
> *nor has anything been kept secret but that it should come to*

light. 23 "If anyone has ears to hear, let him hear." 24 Then He said to them, "Take heed what you hear. With the same measure you use, it will be measured to you; and to you who hear, more will be given.

These verses are all in context to Jesus' teaching of the parable of the Sower. It is given to us, as believers, to know the mysteries or secrets of the Kingdom of God. God is the revealer of things that are hidden and He desires to reveal those things. We need to take heed of what we hear, to learn and discern those voices we hear. The reward will be great when we hear and obey. If we will be faithful in the things we hear from God, then, He will give us more hearing so that we can come more and more into the light of His Kingdom and into His will. Lord, give your children ears to hear what you are saying.

Joseph's Warning to Flee to Egypt

> *Matthew 2:13 Now when they had departed, behold, an angel of the Lord appeared to Joseph in a dream, saying, "Arise, take the young Child and His mother, flee to Egypt, and stay there until I bring you word; for Herod will seek the young Child to destroy Him." 14 When he arose, he took the young Child and His mother by night and departed for Egypt, 15 and was there until the death of Herod, that it might be fulfilled which was spoken by the Lord through the prophet, saying, "Out of Egypt I called My Son." 16 Then Herod, when he saw that he was deceived by the wise men, was exceedingly angry; and he sent forth and put to death all the male children who were in Bethlehem and in all its districts, from two years old and under, according to the time which he had determined from the wise men.*

Joseph did exactly what the Lord said to him in his dream. He rose, he fled, he stayed, and he waited for further instructions. So what happens if Joseph falls back to sleep on this night after the visitation in his dream, and wakes up, and forgets the dream? Or worse, ignores it and chooses to follow his own thoughts? What if he would have awoke and said, "Oh, it was just a dream"? What would have happened to the Christ child? He would have been killed along with all the other male children under two years old.

You and I are holding the life of the Christ Child in our hearts. Are we sustaining that life of Christ in us on the earth? Are we keeping Christ alive through our obedience to his sayings, direction, and warnings?

Joseph's Warning Not to Go to Judea

> _Matthew 2:19 But when Herod was dead, behold, an angel of the Lord appeared in a dream to Joseph in Egypt, 20 saying, "Arise, take the young Child and His mother, and go to the land of Israel, for those who sought the young Child's life are dead." 21 Then he arose, took the young Child and His mother, and came into the land of Israel. 22 But when he heard that Archelaus was reigning over Judea instead of his father Herod, he was afraid to go there. And **being warned by God in a dream, he turned aside into the region of Galilee.** 23 And he came and dwelt in a city called Nazareth, that it might be fulfilled which was spoken by the prophets, "He shall be called a Nazarene."_

Arise and go! Joseph then gets the nod from heaven that it is okay to return to Israel. But as he heads toward Judah, he receives yet another warning to "turn aside." Instead he settles in the region of Galilee. Joseph lived out his dreams from heaven. We should too. It gives life to us and to those around us. Joseph responded to God's every warning and fulfilled Biblical prophesy by his obedience. That is what the Bible is talking about when we pray "Thy will be done, on earth as it is in heaven." My own paraphrasing would suggest thinking of it as on earth as it is "spoken from and done" in heaven. That our lives are to be a simultaneous reflection of what God in heaven is saying and doing.

Warning Dream Given to Pilot's Wife

> *Matthew 27:17 Therefore, when they had gathered together, Pilate said to them, "Whom do you want me to release to you? Barabbas, or Jesus who is called Christ?" 18 For he knew that they had handed Him over because of envy. 19 While he was sitting on the judgment seat, his wife sent to him, saying, "**Have nothing to do with that just Man, for I have suffered many things today in a dream** because of Him." … 24 When Pilate saw that he could not prevail at all, but rather that a tumult was rising, he took water and washed his hands before the multitude, saying, "I am innocent of the blood of this just Person. You see to it."*

Again, here is another example of a non-believer, Pilot's wife, paying attention to her dreams. Certainly, back in those days, people were aware of the significance of dreams and listened to them to a greater degree than we do as Christians in America today. Pilot probably spared himself great trials by listening to his wife's warning prompted by the dream. In response, he washed his hands as a symbolic act of yielding to the Dream-Giver.

Many people say they don't dream. More correctly, they don't remember their dreams as we each dream from three to seven times each night. In our Western Civilization we have not been taught that our dreams are significant. worse yet, we have not been taught in our churches. We discard dreams as being nonsense, certainly not necessary for daily living. I believe this is the farthest from the truth. We need a doctrine for dreams as well as visions, signs and wonders. I would say that we have some catching up to do in this area compared to some psychics and New-age believers. These days I view the unredeemed souls listening to unseen voices differently. May they one day be drawn to the Savior when they hear His voice and no longer listen to another. It does leave me wondering: on Judgment Day how will these two fare by comparison. Unredeemed souls who were listening attentively to any unseen voice, and "so called" saved souls whose hearts have turned away from the diverse means in which God is speaking.

There are of course, so many more scriptural accounts regarding dreams. These chosen are a few examples of the specific warning dreams that can help us learn more regarding this great gift from God. God gave many warnings through dreams in Biblical times and He still does today.

CHAPTER 5

AMERICA'S MOST FAMOUS WARNING DREAM

This Man's Account of an Eerie Dream of Death

"About ten days ago, I retired late. I soon began to dream. There seemed to be a death-like stillness about me. Then I heard subdued sobs, as if a number of people were weeping. I thought I left my bed and wandered downstairs. There, the silence was broken by the same pitiful sobbing, but the mourners were invisible. I went from room to room; no living person was in sight, but the same mournful sounds of distress met me as I passed along."

"It was light in all the rooms; every object was familiar to me, but where were all the people who were grieving as if their hearts would break? I was puzzled and alarmed. What could be the meaning of all this? Determined to find the cause of a state of things so mysterious and so shocking, I kept on until I arrived at the east room, which I entered. Before me was a catafalque, on which rested a corpse wrapped in funeral vestments. Around it were stationed soldiers who were acting as guards; and there was a throng of people, some gazing mournfully upon the corpse, whose face was covered, others weeping pitifully."

'Who is dead in the White House?', I demanded of one of the soldiers." 'The President', was his answer, 'He was killed by an assassin.'"

Then came a loud burst of grief from the crowd, which awoke me from my dream. I slept no more that night; and although it was only a dream, I have been strangely annoyed by it ever since."

A short time after the dream, while attending a performance of a play called "Our American Cousin" at Ford's Theater; President Abraham Lincoln was killed by an assassin named John Wilkes Booth. His body was displayed in the East Room of the White House. His wife Mary would recall this dream of her husband's quite vividly in the days that followed. It was said that her first coherent word after the assassination was a muttered statement about his dream being prophetic. Perhaps the most famous supernatural incident connected to Lincoln was the last prophetic dream of his assassination.

This warning dream of Abraham Lincoln's is well known. A matter of record, it can be found on the Internet very easily along with other "strange" visions and dreams Abraham Lincoln and others close to him had while serving his term. The main point of my book is spelled out quite clearly in the dream of a man holding the highest office in the government of the United States. We do not have a doctrine for dreams, and we need one. A president of the United States dies, and we sit back, not being able to do anything about it. President Lincoln didn't do anything about it. He didn't share it with his pastor as far as it is known. Our pastors don't know what to do with this. We as Christians do not know how to go about "rightly dividing the word of truth" as it speaks of in 2 Timothy 2:15. I prefer the wording in the Revised Standard Version of this verse that states: "*rightly handling the word of truth.*" There is a right way to handle these warnings from heaven as revealed in our dreams.

We are left mystified and suffer the loss of a very famous man and one of our greatest presidents. Did anyone else other than the President hear a warning from heaven regarding this great man's upcoming tragedy? Was this a dream sent by the devil? After all, would a loving God send such a fateful dream to the President days before he was to die? That just doesn't make a lot of sense. There are many typical signs and things to learn from President Lincoln's warning dream. Let's take a closer look.

"About ten days ago... "

He journals the dream, though unfortunately he does this "about ten days" after he had it. There certainly could have been details he missed or things he forgot even though, for the most part, it seems it was one of those dreams not soon forgotten. Even so, generally, we forget most of a dream within ten minutes after waking. Details are the first to go. And they can all be important. With a prophetic warning dream, time is of the essence. We need to take action before the event comes to pass. From my observation, most of the time warning dreams will play out that very day of the dream. They can happen within two days, or ten days, and in some cases have come to pass years later.

"It was light in all the rooms"

Here is a telltale sign and indicator that this is a God dream. It has been taught that dreams that have vivid colors are God dreams. While I can't back that up Scripturally, I believe that it is true based upon my God dreams. We can only see things in vivid color in real life when there is a presence of light. The Scriptures do say in 1John 1:5 that "God is light and in Him there is no darkness at all." Watch for vivid color dreams or dreams in which there is an obvious recognition of light in the scene or scenes.

"a death-like stillness about me, subdued sobs, as if a number of people were weeping, pitiful sobbing, sounds of distress, a state of things so mysterious and so shocking, weeping pitifully"

The dreamer observes such a great amount of sadness, crying, grief, and distress in this dream. The dream makes an obvious statement that there is something very wrong here.

"a catafalque [a stand that supports a coffin], on which rested a corpse wrapped in funeral vestments, gazing mournfully upon the corpse"

Again this is obvious when we look at this literally. There is the presence of a stand, which supports a coffin, a corpse with funeral vestments, and a corpse. This is all followed by conversation, which is totally revealing:

"Who is dead in the White House?... The President... He was killed by an assassin."

We need to look at what is spoken in our dreams. God gives knowledge here. He states who is dead, where the body is, and even reveals how the person in the dream dies. It is about as literal as possible and literal dreams don't need much interpretation.

"I was puzzled and alarmed, I slept no more that night"

Our emotions can have a large part to do with warning dreams from God. Emotions can be just as important as the dream itself, whether these emotions are seen or witnessed within the dream or upon waking up from the dream. Lincoln was "puzzled and alarmed" within the dream. Not being able to sleep the rest of the night came as a result of the emotions he had upon waking up. Most warning dreams are quite literal. Every time we dream about someone dying, it doesn't mean it is to be interpreted literally. I believe dreams are mostly symbolic so I start from that perspective. People die in more ways than physically. As Christians, we are called to die to ourselves. It is a spiritual death. We can suffer an emotional death, the death of a hope, a desire, or even experience the death of a relationship. At times, the Lord may want to address these types of deaths in our lives. He may do so in a dream in order to help us in some way. He may do so by showing us our own death, and interpreted correctly, we should find symbolically want God is referring to in our own lives. Most of the time when it is to be interpreted symbolically, we won't have the ill emotions that President Lincoln felt for days afterwards. If a dream is symbolic, we generally don't even see the dream as being frightful. We need to learn the role that our emotions play in our dreams. That comes with the experience of observing many dreams over a period of time.

"although it was only a dream, I have been strangely annoyed by it ever since."

Lincoln was obviously so effected by this dream, he could not shake the thought of it. One reason that the dreamer is so affected emotionally is that, as in this case, he dreamed about his own death. From my experience of hundreds of warning dreams, the dreams are about other people, mostly loved ones. On the other hand, we can't really know if warning dreams prophesying our own death, occur as often because the dreamer, most of the time, is not around to give testimony of the dream. They indeed die without telling anyone about the dream. We come to the phrase in the same sentence of being "strangely annoyed by" the dream "ever since" it occurred. The reason the annoyance persisted is that God was doing His part so that Lincoln would rightly come to understand the dream and respond appropriately so that this event would not come to pass. Once the dreamer responds effectively and faithfully, the annoyed feeling will go away.

"although it was only a dream"

How many times have we heard that one! "It was only a dream." Well this dream just happened to prophesy the impending doom of this man's very short life. This dream came from The Only True God who is the only One who knows what will be; the only One who knows Satan's plans for evil; the only One who loves us so much that he would send ample warning in order for us to avert the disaster that is coming. He is looking for us to take the proper steps to change the course of this future event. President Lincoln's biggest mistake in his life was summed up in that phrase, "It was only a dream". He didn't know God gives warning dreams. Maybe he knew God reveals things through dreams prophetically but didn't know that something could have been done about it. Abraham Lincoln made many famous quotes in his lifetime. The most significant quote in his life, while not so famous, was, "It was only a dream!" What a pity!

CHAPTER 6

GOD IS SPEAKING

Many believers have had dreams and have wondered if the dreams were divinely inspired. While this book is specifically about God's warnings and alerts we receive through dreams, I would be remiss if I didn't help the reader understand, in an abbreviated manner, that God does indeed speak to us today through dreams in general. I will endeavor to show this through the Scriptures as well as through personal observation, personal experiences, and the experiences of many others. I hope to write more thoroughly on the topic of dreams in general in a later book. I also would encourage personal study of the Scriptures to discover how much of the Bible is composed of that which has come to man through dreams and visions.

That We May Have Life More Abundantly

John 10:10 *"The thief does not come except to steal, and to kill, and to destroy. I* [Jesus Christ] *have come that they may have life, and that they may have it more abundantly.*

In context of the Parable of the Good Shepherd, the thief represents the false prophets and teachers who oppose Christ and his message. Nonetheless in John 8:44, two chapters preceding this parable, Jesus was speaking to the Pharisees and told them they were of their father the devil, and they do the will of their father, the devil. Jesus goes on to say that the devil "was a murderer from the beginning". We have an enemy in this life that has one main goal: to steal, kill, and destroy us, theologically, spiritually, emotionally, and physically. That's what he attempts to do. That is always his purpose and plan. He plans and implements assignments for our destruction time after time in our lives and the lives of those that are dear to us. He never ceases in searching to find an open door to our destruction.

Conversely, Christ is the answer to these assignments of murder and destruction. God comes to us through His only Son sent to earth to die for our sins and reconcile us to Himself. Christ, now ascended, sent the Holy Spirit to come and live within us. However, we see those who believe on Christ being robbed. We see their lives destroyed in many various ways. We see premature death in the saints and in the lost. So, where is this life and life more abundantly? Can we know the enemy's specific assignments against our loved ones and us before they happen? And, can we cancel or minimize these assignments as we receive prophetic warnings in our dreams? Is this promise of life and life more abundantly conditional on anything beyond simply accepting Christ as Savior and Lord of our lives? I believe it is.

He Has Given Us All Things Pertaining to Life

2 Peter 1: 3 …His divine power has given to us all things that pertain to life and godliness, through the knowledge of Him who called us …

Peter states that the Lord has given us everything that pertains to life and godliness through Christ. From my experience over the years of growing in hearing the Lord's voice, I personally have come to believe and conclude that the Lord is giving mankind every warning concerning our individual lives, lives of our loved ones, as well as the lives of others. In my family we now see this time and time again. It has produced fruit like never before in our lives. The Kingdom of God has manifested beyond what we ever knew or believed possible. These warnings are life sustaining and life giving. The question is, do we have the ears to hear them and the knowledge as to how to respond faithfully to them?

How Did God Speak to the Prophets?

Numbers 12:6 Then He said, "Hear now My words: If there is a prophet among you, I, the LORD, make Myself known to him in a vision; I speak to him in a dream."

How did the Lord speak to his prophets? He spoke largely in dreams and visions the author of this passage says. In reading the books of the prophets I never really thought of *how* the Lord spoke to them. When it says, "the Lord told Isaiah", *how* do we assume He told him? We tend to think that God spoke to Isaiah in the prophet's own native language. Many times the Lord used angels to speak to the prophets, but even then, there are many recorded times in the Bible where angels appeared to people in dreams. This verse says God spoke to the prophets through dreams and visions. God used symbolic language in these dreams. These prophets needed to pay attention to their dreams, accurately interpret them, and then in turn, give the prophetic Word of the Lord to the people.

Psalms 19: 1 The heavens declare the glory of God; And the firmament shows His handiwork. 2 Day unto day utters speech, And night unto night reveals knowledge. 3 There is no speech nor language where their voice is not heard. 4 Their line has gone out through all the earth, And their words to the end of the world.

Day after day and night after night the Lord is speaking and revealing truth and knowledge from heaven to the earth by many various means. Not just dreams, of course. We should be very able to see God in His creation itself. These declarations are given to all peoples of all languages regardless of one's belief in God. Those who receive God's words are those with ears to hear his voice. I am not suggesting that each person is called to hear everything that God is saying. That's why we have the body of Christ. But I do suggest that there is so much more to be heard, especially the things that are life giving to us individually. Thus, day and night, the Lord is revealing to us through many means: His glory, His handiwork, His knowledge, His uttered speech, His voice, His line [sound], and His words.

Romans 10:18 … Their sound has gone out to all the earth, and their words to the ends of the world.

The apostle Paul quotes the essence of Psalm 19 in Romans 10:18 saying, "Their *sound* has gone out to all the earth, and their words to the ends of the world." Here the word "sound" is used in most translations in the New Testament instead of "line" giving us better clarification that sounds are indeed coming out of heaven to all the ends of the world. Let's not do away with the word line though. I like that picture. We have a direct "line" of communication with our God through Christ. If we would spend more time on line with God as we do these days on our cell phones with other people, we would be better off.

How Does God Speak To Us Today?

Hebrews 1:1 God, who at various times and in various ways spoke in time past to the fathers by the prophets, 2 has in these last days spoken to us by His Son, …

In the Old Testament times, the Lord declared His Word to man predominately through his servants the prophets. God is unchanged and today, in these last days, God speaks to us through The Prophet, Jesus. Take a look now at how God said His Son would speak to us in these last days.

Acts 2: 17 'And it shall come to pass in the last days, says God, That I will pour out of My Spirit on all flesh; Your sons and your daughters shall prophesy, Your young men shall see visions, Your old men shall dream dreams. 18 And on My menservants and on My maidservants I will pour out My Spirit in those days; And they shall prophesy. 19 I will show wonders in heaven above And signs in the earth beneath: Blood and fire and vapor of smoke.

We have been in the last days since the day of Pentecost. And we have The Prophet living in each and every believer through the Holy Spirit. It is the Spirit of Christ. These verses declare that dreams, visions, prophesies, sign and wonders will be the evidence of this pouring out of His Spirit upon *all* flesh. He is available to all, regardless of age, sex, race or religion. It is also His means of drawing near to unbelievers and bringing them to the saving knowledge of His Son, Christ Jesus.

The Aspects of the Holy Spirit

The real problem in Christendom is that we have not been indoctrinated in respect to prophesy, dreams, visions, signs, and wonders, "The Outpourings of the Holy Spirit". Many Christians have embraced "The Gifts of the Holy Spirit" (1 Corinthians 12:4-11) as being for today. Many have accepted "The Offices of the Holy Spirit" (1 Corinthians 12:28). All Christians know the "Fruit of the Holy Spirit" (Galatians 5:22). But, very few have embraced and turned their ears and eyes and hearts heavenward to "The Outpourings of the Holy Spirit" (Acts 2:17-19).

Of course, there are those in the body of Christ who have embraced prophecy as a valid means of God speaking to individuals or the Church. I ask why and how can we accept, believe, and function in one of these outpouring manifestations of the Holy Spirit and neglect and deny the importance and validity of the others. I asked the Lord for understanding as to why "prophesy" and not the others? In my personal study of The Outpourings, I first noticed that prophecy is the only outpouring that is also a Gift of the Holy Spirit. I wondered and pondered that and realized the difference between Outpourings and Gifts have to do with delivery. Outpourings are messages from heaven to Earth, God speaking directly to man. The Gifts are God speaking through man, *to* man, from earth to earth if you will. Thus, the Outpouring of prophesy is a direct word given from God in heaven to man as with in a dream, and the Gift of prophesy is man relating that prophetic word or message to fellow man as the Spirit wills and directs.

Certainly God speaks to us through that still small voice we hear within us from time to time. Yes, God speaks to us as we read the Scriptures or other Christian books, as well as an inspired sermon or teaching. But God is not limited to those means. God is able, through dreams, to address the issues we are facing or will face in our everyday life. By dreams God can give us direction, instruction, revelation, and warnings that all will bring a better future if we heed them.

CHAPTER 7

HE WILL TELL YOU THINGS TO COME

John 16:12 *"I still have many things to say to you, but you cannot bear them now. 13 "However, when He, the Spirit of truth, has come, He will guide you into all truth; for He will not speak on His own authority, but whatever He hears He will speak; and **He will tell you things to come.** 14 "He will glorify Me, for He will take of what is Mine and declare it to you. 15 "All things that the Father has are Mine. Therefore I said that He will take of Mine and declare it to you.*

My First Experience of Things To Come

When I was eighteen years old, I had a number of like visions concerning the rock band I was in. I was yet unsaved, but I would envision our band living at a lake cabin and writing and playing music. I saw the cabin on a hill and set back from the lake. I also would see this room in the cabin with a large fireplace and a curved couch in front of it. I didn't have an answer for why I kept seeing these images and deduced it was a figment of my imagination. These pictures and scenes would come to me spontaneously without my effort or thoughts. Within months after these visions of the cabin, I had a revelation of Jesus Christ and a powerful conversion experience. My brother and my cousin, who were both in the band as well, were also converted.

Soon after that, my brother got married. I went with he and his wife to check out a house for rent. It was a four-season lake-home on Lake Nokomis outside of Paynesville, Minnesota. When we drove up to the house, we found it to be on a hill set about fifty yards beyond the lakeshore. It was a one-story mansion once owned by a rich man. Once inside, we were escorted to the living room where the door opened up to a beautiful high-ceilinged room with a six-foot tall fireplace and a very long and curved couch in front of it. My jaw dropped! I was standing in the exact place in the vision I had received over a year previously. My brother and wife secured the place and rented it for nine months. Our former rock band set up our musical gear in the basement, started up a Christian band, wrote our first gospel songs, and practiced on weekends for the next nine months. Other than the band, I had never told anyone about the visions, as I hadn't heard of such a phenomena in the church or American Christianity.

Now we ask the question, is it scriptural and of God that we are given insight to actual events that are to occur in the future? Here in John 16 and the chapters around it, Jesus is close to His time to be crucified. He has assembled his disciples together to give them some instruction as to how things will be once he has departed. Jesus is telling what will happen when the Holy Spirit comes. In verse thirteen He calls the Holy Spirit, the Spirit of Truth. It says that when He, the Holy Spirit comes: 1. He will guide us into all truth 2. He will not speak on His own authority 3. He will speak whatever He hears (from Christ in heaven) and, 4. He will tell us things to come.

He said the Holy Spirit will tell us things to come. In other words, He will tell us about things before they happen. He will prophesy to us things to come in the future. Why? I believe, for our benefit, for the sake of His Kingdom, and for the welfare of the church. He does this sometimes to warn us of impending disaster planned by the enemy to kill, steal, and destroy; for us to do something about it; to be warned, to take the warning, do spiritual warfare, and cut off Satan's plans from coming to pass.

I ask people I teach, "So, what has the Spirit told you recently of the future or future events in your life or events in the world?" Mostly, I get little response. I then tell them that, as a Christian, if you are *not* hearing of any future things or events through the Holy Spirit, then either: 1. Jesus was lying. 2. The Holy Spirit is not functioning as He is supposed to. 3. We aren't paying attention and listening to His voice. It doesn't take but a second to figure out this answer. The purpose of the Lord in speaking to and showing the Holy Spirit things to come, is not for the Spirit's sake but for our sake. It's for the Spirit to relay these things to us in order that we may respond in the appropriate manner and be guided into all the truth. But we have uncircumcised ears and eyes, a large lack of paying attention, and unbelief in what the Word of God says.

> *Daniel 2:28* *"But there is a God in heaven who reveals secrets, and He has made known to King Nebuchadnezzar what will be in the latter days. Your dream, and the visions of your head upon your bed, were these:* *29* *"As for you, O king, thoughts came to your mind while on your bed, about what would come to pass after this; and He who reveals secrets has made known to you what will be.*

God indeed reveals secrets to all people. In these verses the prophet Daniel is in Babylon and comes to the king to interpret his dream. He explains that the dream is concerning "what will be in the latter days", "what would come to pass after this", and that God has revealed, by the dream, "what will be." Could it be made any clearer that God was telling him of things to come? This was a prophetic dream. In verse 46 of the same chapter, Daniel completes his interpretation of the dream by saying, *"The dream is certain, and its interpretation is sure."* Yes, God desires for us to know things to come. Do we have the ears to hear? Do we believe?

He Speaks Prophetically to Us

> *Amos 3:7 Surely the Lord GOD does nothing, unless He reveals His secret to His servants the prophets.*

In the Old Testament times the Lord did not do anything unless he first declared it to man through his servants, the prophets. It is no different today. I have said, through the Holy Spirit we have *"The* Prophet" living in us. Matthew 13:11, in the explanation of parable of the Sower, Jesus tells the disciples, *"It has been given to you to know the mysteries of the kingdom of heaven"*. Another name for mysteries is secrets. Amos says God "reveals His secret".

I believe that these mysteries are given to the whole body of Christ to know today. They come from heaven in many various ways, and they bring the life abundantly that the Lord came to give us. These mysteries come mostly in languages that can only be interpreted with the help of the Holy Spirit dwelling in those who have ears to hear; to those listening and being attentive, who are able to interpret these mysteries, and to those who are obedient in responding appropriately to what God is saying. That should include all who call themselves Christians. We have more work to do in our lives to come to a place in which we are truly abiding in the words from heaven. How many words from heaven have we let drop to the ground by not paying attention to our dreams alone over the years?

God So Loves the World

In our family alone we received three warnings regarding the impending disasters of September 11, 2001. I have previously mentioned the two dreams and the vision we experienced. I often ask this question: Do you think, in the days leading up to 9/11, the Lord said to himself, "One of the greatest disasters in history is coming to America, and I am not going to warn anyone about it." I don't think so. I believe God is love, and He was screaming from heaven the warning to earth on the days and months leading up to that day. He did His part to give us every opportunity to help bring sustained life and salvation from a devastating disaster. He gave us every opportunity to hear from heaven and respond and counter attack this assignment of the enemy to bring heavy destruction and death to so many lives. In the dream classes that I teach, I say that, "If every Christian in this state (that I am teaching in that day) would have been carefully listening to the Lord through their dreams alone, I believe 9/11 never would have happened. By "listening" I mean hearing and responding appropriately to what was heard and interpreted through those dreams.

CHAPTER 8

I BELIEVE! HELP MY UNBELIEF!

Jeremiah 6:10 To whom shall I speak and give warning, That they may hear? Indeed their ear is uncircumcised, And they cannot give heed. Behold, the word of the LORD is a reproach to them; They have no delight in it.

We might say or we have been taught that only God's prophets will see and hear these types of future things from the Lord. Certainly, the Scriptures speak of the office of prophet. But, as I have shown, God's love is so great that He gives prophetic warnings to all of His creation whether they believe in Him or not. He loves everyone. But are we hearing His warnings?

> *Rom 10:17 So then faith comes by hearing, and hearing*
> *by the word of God. 18 But I say, have they not heard? Yes*
> *indeed: "Their sound has gone out to all the earth, And their*
> *words to the ends of the world."*

God *is* speaking, but "have they not heard?" No, we haven't all heard. The body of Christ has heard very little compared to the degree in which we need to hear and to the degree that the Lord is speaking and declaring his love, his mercy and grace to us. His warnings are a part of the life and godliness He is giving us. Sure, we believe that there is a Holy Spirit. But we aren't walking anywhere near to the fullness of the Spirit. I am afraid we have become no better off than the Jews whose ears grew dull resulting in unbelief and disobedience to the Lord as described in the Bible.

Unbelief Operating in The Church

> *Mark 9:17-27 Then one of the crowd answered and said,*
> *"Teacher, I brought You my son, who has a mute spirit…*
> *22 "And often he has thrown him both into the fire and into*
> *the water to destroy him. But if You can do anything, have*
> *compassion on us and help us." 23 Jesus said to him, "If you*
> *can believe, all things are possible to him who believes."*
> *24 Immediately the father of the child cried out and said*
> *with tears, "Lord, I believe; help my unbelief!"*

Everywhere I go to teach and share on dreams and visions, people come up to me and tell me about a prophetic dream about the future that actually came to pass. Many times they say that they have never told this prophetic dream to anyone, including their spouse, and they were afraid to tell anyone about it. They feared telling their pastors and friends. They believed they might be looked upon as being off base, influenced by the devil, or crazy. Many have been shamed and looked down upon for revealing such things in and to the church. So, it remains a hidden secret. We don't know what to do with these dreams. Because of a lack of teaching in our doctrine we keep silent and confused. It is believed by some that this is the realm of the devil, New Age and/or psychic phenomena. I often ask people, "Where in the Bible does it ever say that the devil gave anyone a dream?" In addition, many of our "God dreams" have been cast off as "eating too much pizza" the night before. In my early twenties I had a pastor-friend who, every time I asked him about a significant dream I had, would reply with this very statement; "eating too much pizza".

When I teach, people will ask me about this pizza dream response to their dreams. I have come to call this response, "A spirit of unbelief". We in the church are *filled* with this same unbelief concerning the mysteries of God. I liken this to the man who had a son with a mute spirit and who brought the son before Jesus. When Jesus questioned the man's faith the man replies, "Lord, I believe; help my unbelief!" Herein lies a problem. We believe; but we are also filled with unbelief! The written Word testifies of dreams and visions being a means by which the Holy Spirit operates in our lives, yet we don't believe that.

We don't believe it because we haven't been taught it. It has no place in our doctrinal beliefs. We say we believe the Bible is true when really, we don't believe everything in it because of our unbelief and lack of indoctrination of these truths and realities.

Unbelief among God's Chosen People

> *Matthew 2:1 Now after Jesus was born in Bethlehem of Judea in the days of Herod the king, behold, wise men from the East came to Jerusalem, 2 saying, "Where is He who has been born King of the Jews? For we have seen His star in the East and have come to worship Him." 3 When Herod the king heard this, he was troubled, and all Jerusalem with him. 4 And when he had gathered all the chief priests and scribes of the people together, he inquired of them where the Christ was to be born. 5 So they said to him, "In Bethlehem of Judea, for thus it is written by the prophet: 6 'But you, Bethlehem, in the land of Judah, Are not the least among the rulers of Judah; For out of you shall come a Ruler Who*

will shepherd My people Israel.'"

Let's go back to this story of the wise men going to see the baby Jesus. These magi stroll into the capital Jewish city of Jerusalem asking about the Jew's prophesied Messiah. They probably assumed if anyone should know, it would be those in Jerusalem. Surely these Jews would have known and seen the star; would know the whereabout of their own Messiah! So the whole city, including King Herod, got very troubled. They were all caught off guard. The king asks the heads of the Jews, "What's up with this?" They tell him the Christ would be born in Bethlehem. Now Jerusalem has been alerted by these magi. None of the Jews even go or follow these men to check out the Star in the East? The king seemed to be more concerned than even the Jews, yet he didn't send any official troops or spies out. If this isn't a bad case of unbelief, what is?

Healing of Cancer Through a Dream

An illustration of this type of unbelief comes to mind about my son's former percussion teacher. Luis is a believer, and over the period of a year, we became close. We would share our love of Christ regularly. Early on I shared with him that I do biblical teachings. One day he asked me what I taught and I replied, "Dreams". I could tell by his response that he was quite skeptical.

Soon after he moved away to Iowa. A pastor in the city Luis lived contacted me. This pastor had been to a dream class of mine in Illinois and asked if I could come speak at his church regarding dreams and visions. I accepted and contacted Luis about the engagement. Luis said he and his wife Leo would attend the meetings. He invited my wife and I to come stay overnight at their house the last night of my speaking. My wife and I went to his house late that Sunday evening. They treated us to fabulous Mexican food which they had prepared. They shared what they thought of the meetings. Then Luis said, "My wife was healed of terminal cancer through a dream many years ago!" He and his wife shared the story of how she was diagnosed and sent home to die.

She only had weeks to live. One night she was not feeling well at all and hadn't received much sleep. Finally, she had fallen a sleep. In a dream she simply heard a voice say, "Isaiah sixty, verse one!" She woke up immediately from the dream and grabbed her Spanish Bible. She opened it to the verse to find the words, *"Arise, shine; For your light has come! And the glory of the LORD is risen upon you."* She told us she then got up out of bed and was instantly healed! This was at about 5:00 in the morning. She showered and went to the kitchen to prepare breakfast for her family. She has been healthy and healed of cancer to this day many years later.

They finished telling us the testimony. I looked at Luis and said, "And *yet* you were skeptical and questioned the validity of the dream ministry I am in, and now you are reminded of your wife being healed of cancer through a dream?" We all laughed. Yet this type of unbelief is what remains prevalent in the church today. Here his wife was completely healed of cancer, yet they still were skeptical about dreams because it wasn't taught in the church. No doctrine! Individually, we are convinced of the God given dreams and visions in our own lives at times, but as a whole, question this as a means of God operating in other's lives within the body of Christ.

There is one last note concerning Luis and his family. I had been to Luis and Leo's home once previous to the nights of teaching in that community. It had been about four months earlier. While there, I met their youngest son, Michael, who was in his mid thirties. Luis stated that Michael has had so many dreams. He was even called "the big dreamer" by the rest of his siblings, all of whom were serving the Lord but were skeptics concerning their brother's dreams. As Michael shared with me, it became quickly evident that this young man had many prophetic dreams. At one point he stopped and said that he had met me before. Of course our paths had never crossed until that day. Then he asked me if I gave out binders with a class curriculum. I responded that I did. He then said that he had seen these binders and had been to a class of mine in a dream. Michael attended one of my meetings when I later came back to teach on dreams at a local church. I was the first man in Michael's life to tell him he wasn't crazy and that these prophetic dreams were from God and not Satan.

We must repent of this unbelief and receive the doctrine of these mysteries in which God operates today, just like in biblical times. It is of the utmost importance if we are going to abide in God and in His kingdom on earth.

Brittany's Two Car Accident Dreams

I have a niece named Brittany. She was about eighteen years old when she woke from a warning dream in which she was in a car accident. She had known that her uncle was into dreams, but she didn't really believe that God operated that way even though she was a believer. The very day of the dream, she was in a car accident. Fortunately, it wasn't a bad one, and she managed to come away with just minor damage to her car. The good news was that she started taking dreams a little more seriously. Over the years she would e-mail me her dreams and many of them were prophetic.

Then one night, years later while away at college she dreamed she was again in a car accident. This time she woke up and prayed as I had taught and also alerted her mom about the dream that morning. Later in the day she found herself riding in a car driven by her roommate. The Lord brought the dream to her remembrance. She began praying immediately. About sixty seconds later a man in a car went through an intersection and their car t-boned the man's car at about forty miles per hour. They impacted the man's car just in front of his driver's side door and totaled the man's car. The man was not injured. Her roommate was fine and Brittany got a scratch on her knee. When they got out of the car, they went to check out the damage on their vehicle and found only a scratch on the front bumper. They were able to drive away from the accident that left the man's car completely totaled. I would say the Lord answered her prayers. In this case, she wasn't able to pray off the whole accident, but witnessed a miracle with her friend's car sustaining only a small scratch. Days later her parents drove to the city and verified that the car was not damaged. I would call that a loving God who answers prayer. Brittany has been transformed from unbelief to believing, and it continues to have a profound impact on her life.

Romans 10:16 … For Isaiah says, "Lord, who has believed our report?" 17 So then faith comes by hearing, and hearing by the word of God.

Limiting Your Hearing to the Written Word

We need to believe in God's written Word. We also need to believe in the words from heaven. Jesus is the Word. He's the Living Word. We need to learn how to hear his voice and not be unbelieving. Faith comes by hearing, and we many times forget about hearing through the means of the sent Holy Spirit. Yes, the Holy Spirit inspires us as we read the Bible. God reveals himself to us through the written Word. We can't neglect the Living Word that comes to us through the Holy Spirit. The Bible did not tell our family that disaster would strike on September 11th of 2001. Nor did it reveal to me that my children's lives were in danger by the enemy's assignment to take them out via a car accident. The Bible didn't prophesy the specific car accidents to Brittany. No, that was the Holy Spirit doing what it hears and sees from heaven. It was The Word coming through loud and clear through the outpourings of the Spirit. The Bible can't do that! We have limited the power of God by limiting Him in speaking to us only through the Bible. I have seen many a pastor raise his or her Bible high in the air from behind the pulpit and proclaim, "This book is all we need!" I am afraid that is not true. Jesus did not say, "I will send you the Holy Bible!" Jesus said He would send us "the Helper, the Holy Spirit, whom the Father will send in My name". He continued by saying that He, the Holy Spirit, *"will teach you all things and bring to your remembrance all things…"*. We need to pay attention desperately to the voice of God in all the various ways in which He is speaking to us, and believe when He does speak to us. Faith comes by hearing and hearing comes by the Word of God. Lord, help my unbelief!

CHAPTER 9

IDENTIFYING THE ENEMY

1John 2:27 "But the anointing which you have received from Him abides in you, and you do not need that anyone teach you; but as the same anointing teaches you concerning all things, and is true, and is not a lie, and just as it has taught you, you will abide in Him."

Interpreting God's Warning Dreams

The Holy Spirit is the interpreter of the mysteries of God. God can teach how to interpret dreams and the mysteries that God speaks. The anointing of the Holy Spirit can and is willing to help interpret all things. Yes, we need the body of Christ. Yes, we can miss the truth by our own biases and selfish ambitions. Yes, some may be better than others in interpreting various mysteries from God. However, the Lord wouldn't give people dreams and visions if it weren't possible for them to interpret them with some degree of efficiency.

> *Jeremiah 29:13 And you will seek Me and find Me, when you search for Me with all your heart.*

It takes discipline to learn the language of dreams. Like most things, it takes practice. We are to seek ye *first* the Kingdom of God. With perseverance, understanding of what the Lord is revealing through his mysteries will occur.

I am not going to go into an exhaustive teaching on interpreting dreams in this book. My intent is to help you understand what warning dreams look like specifically. The reason we can jump to warning dreams is that generally warning dreams are easier to interpret than most other "God dreams". Most dreams come to us in parables. They are in symbolic language. We understand and use language to some extent in our lives. Unfortunately, we are literalists, and we have not learned to think or look at things symbolically in order to understand most dreams. The good news is that while a warning dream may have symbolism in it to some degree, there are other identifiable literal things going on in them that can help us know when we have them.

The following will help identify warning dreams if one is received. Keep in mind that these helps are general statements. There can be variations or differences in a warning dream experienced. Just because a dream has some of the elements I mention in this chapter, doesn't necessarily mean it's a warning dream.

I will present pictures and ideas that may be common indicators in warning dreams. Please don't take these examples as absolutes in trying to interpret dreams. They are meant to give a better understanding of what needs to be watched. There can be exceptions and variations to everything I describe. I am not trying to make things simple for the dreamer. It takes the Holy Spirit's operation to help us walk in a healthy way concerning our dreams. Please keep that in mind in this chapter.

1Peter 5:8 Be sober, be vigilant; because your adversary the devil walks about like a roaring lion, seeking whom he may devour.

Feelings

What is sensed within the dream can greatly help in identifying a warning from heaven. The presence of evil may be sensed. Generally, one will become fearful in the dream, quite possibly extremely fearful. These feelings will come with heightened emotions. The dreamer may be awakened with a realization that the dream was about trouble and no good. This may leaves the dreamer shaken, sweating, frightened, crying, or greatly moved emotionally. However, we will also dream fearful dreams based upon our fears. Ultimately, the dreamer must learn to distinguish these feelings in a warning dream from everyday fears.

Attacks

One of the next things to look for is an attack in the dream. For example, this can come from things like animals, people, or manned objects such as helicopters, jets, or vehicles.

Animal Attacks

The dreamer may be attacked by an animal in a warning dream. These can be any type of animal. Common ones are snakes, dogs, spiders, or bats to name a few. Animals generally represent spirits in dreams. It is possible to name the force that is coming against the dreamer by the attacking animal that in the dream. Interpreting and knowing what demonic spirit is attacking can be helpful in effectively dealing with it. This will give a better aim at the enemy when prayed against. For instance, my friends and I heard a person tell a dream about a group of crows attacking a group of people in a field. That next day I did some research and found that a group of crows is called "a murder". Thus, being attacked by a group of crows could quite likely represent a spirit of "murder". Again, that may not always mean a physical death. Warning dreams can speak of impending emotional or spiritual death as well. None-the-less, my learning has shown that knowing what exact spirit the animal attacking represents is not absolutely necessary in order to take authority over them. Just observing an attack can be sufficient for recognizing that the Lord is revealing Satan is coming to kill, steal, or destroy in some way or magnitude.

People Attacks

Many times an attack can come from a person in the dream. This person may be known or unknown to the dreamer. This person will be attacking the dreamer or another known person. Evil will likely be sensed. The attacker may be carrying some weapon and there will be knowledge that the intended victim is in danger. If it is the dreamer being attacked, when he wakes up, he will want to ask himself if he feels like someone or something is attacking him in some way in his life. The dreamer may be running from some issue present in his life. There is a need to understand what obsessive fears one has, and learn to distinguish a warning dream from a dream that is a direct result of ones specific fears. If the dreamer is unable to link the fears in the dream symbolically to things going on within his heart or life, then he may have had a warning dream.

Manned Object Attacks

If one is under attack by some type of manned object, the dreamer could be receiving a warning from heaven. Many times these could come as military objects like helicopters, fighting jets, or any other type of military vehicle. These can signify spiritual warfare. The dreamer may observe shots fired at them or another person known by the dreamer. Conversely, shots fired can symbolically reveal that a certain person or people are talking bad about the dreamer. That would not necessarily mean it is a warning dream. It could instead be a revelation dream which may be God revealing paranoid thoughts. Indeed it could be a revelation that someone is speaking evil or gossiping about the dreamer.

Accidents

Another type of dream that may indicate God's giving a warning dream is by witnessing an accident. Again, the accident will be happening to the dreamer and/or others. It could be a car accident or any type of accident. You will generally be stirred by this type of dream and may experience the feelings mentioned previously. Generally, the type of accident will be similar to the actual occurrence that the enemy will be using in his attempt to bring harm to the dreamer of his loved ones. These can be quite literal dreams. The accident in the dream many times will be played out in real life if you don't respond to it. But again, just because you witness a car accident, it doesn't mean that the warning is literally about a car accident. It could be something like a car accident, and a car accident is simply the best way for God to describe the event to you.

Injury or Death

Sometimes the injury or death of a person will be witnessed. This can be a telltale sign of impending danger. You will know that someone has died or has been injured. This will probably be accompanied by heightened emotions or an evil presence. Many times the Lord will give us dreams that include ourselves or others dying or being dead. Don't forget that it could be a representation of one going through a spiritual death of some kind. We need to identify with Christ's death as Christians. Many times this is revealed by a physical death in a dream. As you get better in dream interpretation, you will be better able to discern the difference. If it is a representation of a spiritual death, many times you won't feel horrified as if it were something really bad or evil. I will explain later healthy ways to respond to dreams that concern other people, what to do about them, and with whom to share the information.

Angels

> *Daniel 8:15 Then it happened, when I, Daniel, had seen the vision and was seeking the meaning, that suddenly there stood before me one having the appearance of a man. 16 And I heard a man's voice between the banks of the Ulai, who called, and said, "Gabriel, make this man understand the vision."*

Like an angel telling Joseph to flee to Egypt with Mary and the baby Jesus, an angel may appear to warn you in your dream. Don't be looking for an angel with wings. This is probably the least way that they reveal themselves to you. An angel will, more than likely, look like a regular person. The dreamer will probably call them "a stranger". The angel may tell you something you need to know or even escort you somewhere to show you something that needs your attention and response. Even the archangel Gabriel appeared to Daniel the prophet as a man.

Other Signs of Warning

Other ways to identify Satan coming to harm someone is by a simple evil presence. Someone may be observed in a casket, or the dream will take place at a funeral. The dreamer may just have a knowing that a certain person is in trouble in the dream. We may have never really thought about it, but many times in our dreams we just know something without seeing it. There can be many other indicators to lead us to believe that something is very wrong in our dreams. God will make every attempt to make it clear enough to know pr suspect the dream to be a warning. Over time, these things won't very hard to discern, and they could save the dreamer's life, the life of a loved one, or at least save one from harm or heartache.

I can't emphasize enough that any of these types of dreams mentioned above may be merely symbolic dreams that may not be warnings from heaven. That is okay. We all need to err on the side of caution in most every case with these types of dreams. I would rather be safe than sorry, and so would you. It isn't worth misinterpreting a dream like this. To this day, almost without exception, I will err on the side of caution with warning dreams. Remain watchful.

Call the Authorities!

Hebrews 4:16 Let us therefore come boldly to the throne of grace, that we may obtain mercy and find grace to help in time of need.

Along with all the signs previously mentioned, one should also get a hint that God is alerting or warning when someone calls the authorities in the dream. Many times in the dream, the dreamer or someone will be told to call 9-1-1, or to "get help" or "call the police". That is many times symbolic for calling on God in prayer for help in time of need. We know that we dial 9-1-1 for an emergency. In these dreams, God is revealing an emergency in some area of our life or the life of another. This is a clear sign to pray as soon as you wake from the dream. It isn't hard to interpret a dream with a scene of calling for help. Know that there is reason to pray to our Authority in heaven. Even if you don't know who or what to pray for, or you are unable to understand the dream, you will understand it needs spiritual attention. Tell God to help on behalf of the dream you just had. Pray the dream even without understanding the symbolism.

Nightmares

Nightmares are not necessarily associated with warning dreams. From my experience, nightmares are prompted from excessive preconditioned fears, anxieties, or being emotionally disturbed in some way in your everyday life. Nightmares generally are prompted by the past and reveal the unredeemed things that are going on in the dreamer's life. Nightmares can be prompted by excessive fears, panic, trauma, and insecurities due to things the dreamer experienced in the past. Nightmares may also be an indication of demonic powers at work in one's life. They are separate from warning dreams in general. If you are experiencing nightmares on a regular basis, you need to address them. The Lord can help you get delivered of them. This is not my area of expertise as I have rarely experienced them in my own personal life. These are not to be mistaken for warning dreams. Most people who have nightmares or night terrors know the difference in context with their life.

I don't know why God just doesn't take care of these things for us, but this is the way it is. He needs our active response to deal with the powers of darkness on this earth. If we learn these laws, we can walk in the life in which He has called our loved ones and us.

CHAPTER 10

BREAKING OFF THE ASSIGNMENT OF THE ENEMY

*Ephesians 6:10 Finally, my brethren, be strong in the Lord and in the power of His might. 11 Put on the whole armor of God, **that you may be able to stand against the wiles of the devil.** 12 For we do not wrestle against flesh and blood, but against principalities, against powers, against the rulers of the darkness of this age, against spiritual hosts of wickedness in the heavenly places. 13 Therefore take up the whole armor of God, **that you may be able to***

withstand in the evil day, and having done all, to stand.
… 17 And take the helmet of salvation, and the sword of
the Spirit, which is the word of God; 18 praying
*always **with all prayer and supplication in the Spirit,***
being watchful to this end with all perseverance and
supplication for all the saints---

Breaking Off the Assignment of the Enemy

I want to make it as simple as I can to identify and cancel the enemy's attack should anyone receive a warning dream from God. Responding correctly could be the difference between life and death. There is no set formula for doing this. The main thing is to respond in faith when it is believed that God has revealed "the wiles of the devil" with his "fiery darts". The object of this is to make sure it does *not* come to pass as He has revealed it. He has given us all the tools to "withstand in the evil day". We just need to walk out our part and be faithful to respond.

As the verse says, we need to withstand the evil day. The Evil Day is bound to come. No one is exempt from The Evil Day. This is the day that the forces of darkness have targeted the dreamer or his loved ones for destruction. Satan's wish is to steal our joy. He wants to hinder our walk with God in any way he can. He is out to destroy our lives and if possible, steal our loved ones from us. I don't know how many times in one's life The Evil Day comes to literally kill us, but I don't want to miss being ready on that day. So, be watchful! Be ready! I don't want to see anyone I love die prematurely. My plea and hope is that people will know what to do if and when that day comes. It may only happen once in a person's life that the evil one comes to perform the ultimate in taking a life of a loved one. Don't miss that one time!

Luke 10:19 "Behold, I give you the authority to trample
on serpents and scorpions, and over all the power of the
enemy, and nothing shall by any means hurt you.

Praying with Our Understanding

When I receive a warning dream from the Lord, I use a certain vernacular in prayer that I am accustomed to using. I want to show what has worked effectively for me; not so much to say a prayer using my exact words, but instead to get the gist of what I am saying. Find the words that will cause you to believe what you are praying. I personally call this response to a warning from God as "breaking off the assignment of the enemy" who comes to steal, kill, or destroy my loved ones, or me. For example, if I dreamed of a snake biting my daughter and not letting go, I would pray, "Lord, I break off the assignment of the enemy to kill or harm my daughter Christine in any way according to the dream you have revealed to me. I come and stand against that snake-like spirit and bind it in the name of Jesus and cancel its attack, in Jesus name, Amen." I then continue in a spirit of prayer and listen for any further prompting of the Spirit. I may even go deeper than that at times. If I can easily identify the snake in the dream, I go to my resources and find out if there is such a snake. I will see if it is a constrictor or a poisonous snake, for instance. If it is a constrictor, I will pray against the enemy's will of constricting my daughter in any way. That it won't be able to choke out the work in God that she is doing. I will pray whatever else I am prompted to pray. If it is a poisonous snake, then I know the enemy is coming in a slightly different way to poison her. I will pray against the venomous spirit that wants to poison her faith, marriage, or whatever else it may be. Again, the main thing is to be led by the Spirit in these prayers of deliverance.

1Corinthians 14:14 For if I pray in a tongue, my spirit prays, but my understanding is unfruitful. 15 What is the conclusion then? I will pray with the spirit, and I will also pray with the understanding.

Praying with the Spirit

Usually I will continue to intercede for my daughter, for

instance, by praying in tongues which is also call "praying with the Spirit" just as verse 18 says in the verses above: *"praying always with all prayer and supplication in the Spirit, being watchful to this end with all perseverance and supplication for all the saints"*. Whether one does or doesn't speak in tongues, and it is not my purpose here to try to convince that tongues are for today or anything in that regard, matters less to me. I happen to believe that it is for today and is a powerful tool for the very purposes of thwarting the enemy. Having said that, more importantly it is the prayer of faith that will deliver from this evil assignment and to a lesser degree, the method of prayer. My concern is that a response is made regardless of what one specifically believes.

> *Romans 8:26 Likewise the Spirit also helps in our weaknesses. For we do not know what we should pray for as we ought, but the Spirit Himself makes intercession for us with groanings which cannot be uttered.*

I also have found it helpful to pray in tongues with many various dreams that prompt me to pray and intercede. Sometimes I do not know just whom it is I am praying for, and what exactly I am praying against, or exactly how to accurately pray against it. I am dependant on and trusting in the Holy Spirit to intercede for me on behalf of the revealed dream. I believe it helps me in my lack of perfect knowledge and interpretation. It gives me a great confidence and adds to my faith and conviction. Jesus called the Holy Spirit the Helper. In these cases I need all His help that I can get.

> *Isaiah 59:19 So shall they fear The name of the LORD from the west, And His glory from the rising of the sun; When the enemy comes in like a flood, The Spirit of the LORD will lift up a standard against him.*

Pray Until a Feeling of Release Comes

The bottom line in praying off the assignment as it has been revealed. Pray in faith and then stop when a release is sensed that you have faithfully obeyed the Spirit. With time one becomes more sensitive his prayer is heard and when he has prayed effectively. Then stand in faith, believing that the work is complete, successfully canceling the assignment of the enemy.

If the Lord brings this dream to remembrance later that day, or any of the days, which follow, it is a call to pray again. The important thing is not to continue in prayers that are prompted by fears. Prayers prompted by fear have little effect as they just reveal a lack of faith. Believe the response on your part has been complete and continue to be watchful for any further promptings of the Spirit.

If the victim in a warning dream is someone known, use discernment and discretion as to whether or not the dream should be told to that person or anyone else. Each case will be different. Sometimes a dream may be shared, and at other times the Spirit makes it clear not to share it. Sometimes I tell the person after a passage of time. Just be obedient. If a mistake is made in this area; learn from that mistake.

Witnessing the "Near Hit"

In the practice of this, the dreamer may see the outward manifestation of the enemy's assignment thwarted. In the case of my "Head-on Collision" warning dream concerning my children, it ended by them missing the collision by a small margin. I witnessed what I call the "near hit" of the warning. If a "near hit" is experience after you have prayed off the assignment, just know that it is to strengthen faith in hearing and interpreting the dream correctly. The Lord has demonstrated the power of prayer and response. This should be of great encouragement and should help in the learning process.

Literal Versus Symbolic

While dreams and visions mostly come to us as parables or in symbolic language, I believe as we grow in our learning and interpreting, we become better at understanding whether a dream is literal or symbolic. I have found on occasion that some dreams can be both symbolic and literal. That is, literally something happens or is true in the natural as well as revealing a symbolic or spiritual truth at the same time. Dreams or visions that have the appearance of being a warning, symbolic or literal, should be handled as if it were literal. Pray off the assignment so you can have abundant life and deliverance.

Erring On the Side of Caution!

Here is where I want to make one of the most significant points of this book. With any apparent warning dream, vision, sign, or wonder that you encounter. "ERR ON THE SIDE OF CAU-TION!" I cannot stress this enough. This is not a science. Writing down all of your dreams is not an absolute necessity in order to do this. Expertise in interpreting dreams isn't the chief thing. If one has a dream that has any signs of evil occurring, then pray off the assignment of the enemy concerning that warning. This could be a matter of life or death. If a dream has been given with any of the signs or scenes that I have explained in detail, and you have a pit in your stomach about the dream when you wake up, *then pray it off*. If we are going to err, then let's err on the side of caution. I don't know for sure all of the times that the dream I get is absolutely a warning from God. If it has the signs of danger, if harm is done to a human being, if the feelings in the dream are horrifying, if some-one dies or is injured, has an illness, or a disease, I will err on the side of caution! No one can afford to be wrong here. We need to cover these dreams with a response and a rebuke. We can't afford to let someone be harmed or killed over us questioning if a dream was really a warning from God or not. Always pray! Always break this off! If you make a practice of listening and paying attention to your dreams, over time, you will get better at detecting whether it is or isn't a warning. When it comes to interpreting my own or oth-ers dreams that may be warnings, I will pray a prayer like this: *"Lord, I come to you on behalf of the dream I had concerning an apparent warning. If this is a literal warning from heaven, then I come against this assignment of the enemy. I break this scheme off and stop it from coming to pass. I cancel this assignment in the name of Jesus, Amen!'"*

> *1John 5:4 For whatever is born of God overcomes the world. And this is the victory that has overcome the world-- our faith.*

I virtually always pray these prayers out loud. I usually continue by praying in tongues over these dreams and keep praying until I feel that release. If you don't speak in tongues, don't worry about it. Speaking in tongues is not that which overcomes the world; it's our faith. It isn't praying and saying all the proper words that give us the victory over the devil's onslaughts; it's our faith. Nor is it having perfect interpretive skills concerning our dreams. You have faith because faith comes by hearing, and when the warning is seen or heard, God gives authority over it and over all the forces that come with it.

If the Lord brings this dream to mind in the hours or days ahead, I will repeat a prayer against this assignment. On most occasions, I don't need to do so. We do need to stand in faith afterwards and not fear or doubt. This praying can last from minutes to hours. Each case is different. But don't pray religious prayers. A religious prayer may be one where one makes it a point to pray this off at every occasion for the next few days. Again, don't pray fear-filled prayers. Pray it off and get on with the day! God is faithful! This is not complicated. These in fact, are the most powerful prayers as faith comes by hearing. We are responding to a simple life-saving warning from heaven. When the scheme or wile of the enemy is withstood, having done all to stand; *then stand!*

CHAPTER 11

RESPONDING APPROPRIATELY

<u>Deuteronomy 29:29</u> "The secret things belong to the LORD our God, but those things which are revealed belong to us and to our children forever, that we may do all the words of this law.

Driving Another Way

A friend sent me a tape series of a man who ministered concerning dreams at a church. When this person talked about warning-type dreams, he mentioned two personal stories. One concerned a dream he had in which he witnessed a car crash on a particular street that he drove often. That day he was to drive on that street but instead took another route to avoid any disaster that may have been waiting for him per the dream. He did not mention, in his teaching, anything about the concept of praying off the assignment of the enemy as it pertains to the warning dream. Like the Magi at the birthplace of Jesus *"they departed for their own country another way,"* (Matthew 2:12), this man chose to take another way to get to his destination. His approach was Scriptural, however, I believe that we don't have to be constantly sidestepping the devil. "Greater is He who is in us, than he that is in the world." Having seen the devil's plan to snare us, I believe that by our faith, which comes by hearing (Romans 10:17) that which the Lord reveals, we can continue on with the Lord's plans for our lives. We can cancel the enemy's assignments. I do want to make it clear that each situation is unique. Walk in faith, and be led by the unction of the Spirit. Indeed, one may just have to avoid a certain path to avoid where the enemy is waiting. In this dream, instead of merely avoiding driving on that street that day, the dreamer could possibly have simply taken authority by faith in what the Lord revealed. He could have cancelled that assignment and confidently driven that street that day and every day thereafter. This dreamer wasn't told in his dream what *day* the crash may happen. It could have been addressing a situation to come two weeks later. He may have forgotten about the dream by then and driven that way. He still might have become a victim of the dream.

Interestingly, while writing this chapter, I got a call from a person who hosts monthly meetings where I teach on dream interpretation. She mentioned a woman at work who is not familiar with this type of teaching. She had a warning dream that her daughter was killed in a car accident. The daughter was planning on returning home from a few states away within the week. This woman told my friend the dream and was shaken over it. Knowing that my friend believes in dreams being from God, this dreamer took my friend's advice and went home with her husband and prayed for their daughter that night concerning the dream. In the end they found airplane flights surprisingly inexpensive and chose to fly her home instead. The daughter made it home safely on the plane. Mission accomplished. Each one of us needs to walk by faith with what God has given us. Then main thing is to respond to the warning according to faith.

Matthew 9:29 Then He touched their eyes, saying, "According to your faith let it be to you."

Snow Skiing Warning

This same dream teacher, also told a story about taking his wife and two sons to Colorado on a skiing trip. They had planned for this trip for quite some time. When they finally arrived, his wife had a warning dream concerning one of their sons being injured on the ski slopes. The boys had been planning on going snow boarding. When she told her husband the dream, they just felt helpless to do anything. They weren't going to be able to keep their sons off the slopes after the long wait to finally be there to ski. They didn't know about breaking off the assignment. They let their sons go out on the slopes that day. Sure enough, one son suffered an accident and broke his arm. What if his son would have died? Thank the Lord it wasn't anything worse. This was sure not a testimony in my mind of the power over the enemy we have as believers. The answer was to pray off such an assignment and enjoy the week God had given them to enjoy. We need to come into a full knowledge of our dreams and how necessary it is to wrestle against the enemy and gain our victory.

On occasion our prophetic warning dreams may be speaking of an event a long time into the future. Most of the time, warning dreams seem to be about something that is imminent, within the next 24 hours, or a few days. But some speak of things a long way off. Either way, we cancel the assignment as we see them.

One November day I was reviewing my dreams, which I do quite regularly. It takes longer and longer to scan through them since I now have well over one thousand of my own dreams recorded and dated from the last eight years. Of course, these are not all God dreams. I had just finished reviewing my dreams a day earlier when my son Paul, who was then a high school senior, came home from school. He had recently become friends with a classmate and told me the boy snowboarded. Paul was wondering if he could buy a snowboard and take up the sport as well as there was a small ski resort only twenty minutes down the road from where we lived. I told him that would be fine, but I expected him the buy the snowboard and equipment with his own money. He no more than left the room when the Holy Spirit brought into my remembrance a dream that I had read in my journal a few days earlier. Upon paging back through my dream journal I came to the following dream I had in May, six months earlier.

The Wake-board Warning

The setting was in the town in which I grew up in. I dreamed I was in a hospital-type building. Many of us were taking showers, and there was a 'code blue'. I saw a doctor running to the Emergency Room. I had a suspicion it was a SARS (Severe Acute Respiratory Syndrome) case. Paul was in the shower room, too. Then we were outside at the bottom of the hill leading to the little store in Long Prairie. I walked with Paul up the hill to the intersection of Todd Street. Todd Street is a side street halfway up this hill. Then Paul took his water board, laid down on it, and proceeded sliding down Todd Street. He quickly slid uncontrollably under a car at an intersection. The side of his head was bruised. Then he again proceeded sliding down the street. I saw he was still a little out of control.

I was shocked! I hadn't remembered interpreting this dream as a warning dream back then, nor did I remember praying off the assignment. I may have, but I just couldn't remember. I wondered why I wouldn't have, as there were too many signs of danger. I was in a hospital, with a "code blue" and a doctor running to the Emergency Room, Paul being half way up a hill, getting hit by a car, suffering some type of head injury, and he was out of control. It had all the signs of a warning dream. In the very least this was a dream to take seriously and "err on the side of caution" by praying! How strange that in my dream Paul was wake-boarding, the real term for boarding on water, down the pavement on a hill in the middle of what seemed to be a summer's day. I then realized, in real life you wake-board on water. What is snow made out of? Water!

Vicky arrived home from teaching school about twenty minutes later, and I told her the story. She and I immediately prayed off the assignment of the enemy to bring harm to our son on the slopes of the ski hill. When we felt like we had prayed through that, I must admit a little fear and anxiety tried to tempt us to doubt. Paul bought the gear he needed over the next couple of days, and I inquired whether or not he purchased a helmet with his gear. He replied that he didn't and explained those were used mostly for going over dangerous moguls, and not while learning to snowboard down the regular part of the hill. I bit my tongue, as he was only months from turning eighteen. He was making a lot of decisions on his own now with his graduation being so close. I didn't pursue it any further, but it did little to help my slight anxiety.

Well, the day arrived. Vicky and I walked Paul to the back door of our house. We had not shared the dream with him as that would have only possibly caused him to fear. We didn't want to put any fear in him. He was a little bewildered when I asked him if I could lay hands on him and pray for his safety and protection before he left. Upon finishing my prayer Paul looked at us and said, "It's no big deal. I am just going to be practicing on the bunny hill trails that are half way up the hill." That should have calmed us, but I knew all too well from the dream that Paul sustained the head injury when he went down the side street which was only "half way" up the hill. We hugged him, told him we loved him, and waved to him as he left for the hills. It was a very difficult moment for us, and I believe we even threw up a couple quick fear-filled prayers (that really don't have a lot of power to them). Mostly we stood in faith, believing that our loving God is faithful and that we had been faithful to respond the way He had taught us.

Paul came home happy and uninjured. Praise the Lord! We could have told Paul not to go. Then wouldn't we have to tell him to hang up his snowboard permanently? How do we know the dream referred to just his first time out? I don't believe we have to succumb to the rule and schemes of the enemy. Whatever we do, we do in faith. We take up the whole armor of God that we may be able to *"withstand in the evil day and having done all, to stand."* I was certainly grateful that dream I had six months earlier caught my attention when I reviewed my dreams that day.

CHAPTER 12

JESUS CAME TO SAVE

In the fall of 1973 my life was falling apart. At least from an eighteen year old's perspective it was. I lost my girlfriend, our rock band broke up, and I was getting deeper into drugs. I failed to show up for my first day of college. My brother and I were living in a rented farmhouse with no refrigerator or stove. I was working the graveyard shift washing dishes at the nearby truck stop. Lost, desperate, and depressed, I prayed that if there were a God that He would reveal Himself to me. Within a month, I came to a saving revelation of Jesus Christ. He brought peace to a life filled with chaos. This experience happened to me in the farmhouse. There was no altar call, no television evangelist's urging, no church involvement what-so-ever. No person was there to tell me I could have a personal relationship with Jesus Christ by turning my life over to Him, nor had I picked up a Christian tract containing the four spiritual laws of how to get saved. All those things may be effective in a person coming to life in Christ, but none of them was the case with me. I had no idea how to "get saved" or what that even meant. It was just me, sitting on a single mattress on a floor and petting a kitten. I was all alone. Suddenly, something like lightening from heaven struck me on the top of my head. I was instantly filled with something from head to toe. I heard a voice in my heart speak loudly and clearly: "I am Jesus Christ. I have come into your heart and into your life"! This was good!

I wasn't even looking for or interested in being saved with the assuredness of eternal life. That meant little to me. My motive for having a relationship with God was not to obtain eternal salvation when I died. I needed a Savior to save me out of the desperate hour I was in presently. I needed some meaning in my life. I needed to know the truth. I couldn't even think much beyond that. I needed help in this life, and that's why I had been seeking God for in the month leading up to this day. Later, finding out that eternal life was included in this was just frosting on the cake. I need to be saved everyday. I live with that mindset as well as the assurance of eternal life.

> *John 12:46* "*I have come as a light into the world, that whoever believes in Me should not abide in darkness.* *47* "*And if anyone hears My words and does not believe, I do not judge him; for I did not come to judge the world but to save the world.* *48* "*He who rejects Me, and does not receive My words, has that which judges him--the word that I have spoken will judge him in the last day.*

Jesus came to save us, both eternally and out of each and every day. I need to make it through *today*! I have a Savior that will help me do that. Jesus loves us. He is not here to judge us. He came to earth to save us and abide in us every day of our life. Theses verses in John, at first glance, puzzled me. As I broke them down they made sense. It is not Jesus who judges us. It's His words that He has spoken that will judge us if we reject them. We need to pay attention and hear His words, believe in what He says, and then faithfully respond to what he has said. Jesus comes and brings life giving words to us, not only through the Bible, but also through the preached word and His words brought to us through the Holy Spirit. The Outpourings of the Spirit brings Christ's words to us. If we don't respond to His saving words, His words will judge us for not listening to them. In other words, He brings warnings, and it will be as judgment if we fail to hear and respond obediently. He reveals the enemy's wiles and schemes coming against us and gives us the opportunity for us or others to be saved out of them. What a loving God! What a reason to be paying attention to the ways the Lord brings His words to us. We need to repent for all His words that we have let fall to the ground. We need to pay attention to the words He brings as they are life saving and life giving.

Sleeping with Our Eyes Open

> _Luke 12: 35_ "Let your waist be girded and your lamps burning; _36_ "and you yourselves be like men who wait for their master, when he will return from the wedding, that when he comes and knocks they may open to him immediately. _37_ "Blessed are those servants whom the master, when he comes, will find watching. Assuredly, I say to you that he will gird himself and have them sit down to eat, and will come and serve them.

Our Master Jesus comes to us in the night and knocks on our door through our dreams. He brings messages that save and give life. We would do well to have our waist girded which means to make ready and be prepared. In the previous chapter, Jesus tells the disciples, "the lamp of the body is the eye". We are exhorted to have our lamps burning throughout the night. Our family has learned to sleep with our eyes open! Of course, we are talking about our spiritual eyes. These are the eyes of our heart.

Every time you wake up in the night it is likely that the Lord has awakened you out of a dream so that you may immediately make note of it and respond to it accordingly. If I am awakened out of a sleep with a warning dream, I immediately get up and head for the living room where I get on my knees in front of the couch. I normally get there within seconds after I wake up. I want to show my master that I am ready to serve Him first in my life. I want to show Him that I believe in these verses in Luke, and I want to honor Him in obedience. I am there at His service. Now He is ready to hear my intercession to Him in response to the warning He has brought through my dream. He answers my prayer and deals with the enemy. Mission accomplished! I want Him to say, "Well done good and faithful servant." I am eternally grateful for the salvation He has brought out of His love for his Creation. He *has* saved the world! Have we responded to His saving grace? Do you wait with lamps burning for your master to come to you in the night? Begin now!

CHAPTER 13

GENERAL WARNINGS

> *Job 33:15 In a dream, in a vision of the night, When deep sleep falls upon men, While slumbering on their beds. 16 Then He opens the ears of men, And seals their instruction. 17 In order to turn man from his deed, And conceal pride from man, 18 He keeps back his soul from the Pit, And his life from perishing by the sword.*

God sends us messages through dreams for many reasons. Verse 18 reveals that He sends a dream to help man keep his soul from the pit and from perishing. It is clear, and it makes so much sense that a loving God would do so for those whom He created and loves. Fortunately, not all warning dreams concern life-threatening circumstances. God sends warnings for even the smallest of things. He is concerned about our lives on every level. Make no mistake, He sends warnings for our own good no matter how insignificant they may seem to us nor whether we are paying attention or not.

Repetitive Dreams

Many people have repetitive dreams and wonder why. Repetitive dreams are characterized by the same main theme, many of the same elements, maybe with a slightly different twist in each one. In general, God gives us repetitive dreams because we are not getting the message. He has to keep sending the dream until we get it. Once we get the message and make the adjustment God is desiring in our life, the dream will go away. Unfortunately, we can have these dreams our whole lives without recognizing what the Lord is saying, and many times to our deficit. The Lord will use repetitive dreams to alert us and warn us about impending problems that need correction, deliverance, or adjustments in our lives.

The Lost Billfold Dream

One day I was talking to a man about dreams. The subject of repetitive dreams came up. I was explaining that for the most part we have the same or similar dream over and over because we are not dealing with a reality in our lives to the proper extent. God can bring us this similar dream time after time to alert us in this regard. The man then said, " Oh, that's like when you have the same dream over and over again that you are losing your billfold and can't find it." I responded,

"Well no," I responded. "I don't have repetitive dreams of losing my billfold." He assumed everyone had this repetitive dream. A few days later I emailed him the interpretation to his billfold dreams. I said in the interpretation, "You have a problem. You are losing money; a lot of it; and you don't even really understand where it went. Furthermore, if you don't remedy this situation you will continue to lose your money." I learned later this same man, who was in his early seventies, had indeed lost all his money over the previous few years--well into the six figures. He mentioned he was now in credit debt. About a year later he filed bankruptcy. Just think. If he would have been able to interpret this dream years earlier, he could have made proper adjustments in order to be more fiscally responsible. I believe the Lord could have revealed the plan for him to make the adjustment as well as simply revealing the problem.

Brittany's Dad is Dead

As mentioned previously, not all warning dreams are literal. A dream of someone dying does necessarily not mean they are dying physically. Here is a case in point.

Brittany woke up one morning from a dream in which her father had died. She told her mother about it right away as she had the dreams about the two car accidents in the recent past. Her mother e-mailed me the story, and I told them to intercede for Jeff, the father, in light of the dream, "erring on the side of caution", should it be a literal dream of an assignment against his very life. They did so. They got back to me that evening with the story of what took place. That very afternoon the bank had called Jeff. Jeff had recently applied with the bank to refinance the house. The bank had called to inform him that upon checking out his credit report, they found on one of the enquires for the application, that Jeff was actually listed as deceased.

So Brittany's dad *was* "dead" in a way, according one of the reports. Fortunately it was *not* a warning dream about an impending life-threatening situation or assignment of the enemy. Their prayers might have in fact also warded off such a potential attack on his life as well. Instead Brittany was shown, through a dream, about a thing to come by the Holy Spirit that concerned her dad's credit report information. Actually I term this one as an alert as there was already an existing problem; it just wasn't brought to their attention until that afternoon. Why she was given that information may be unclear, though it was a continued lesson for this young girl that the Holy Spirit is real and does tell us things to come. It took Jeff months to clear up this mess. It's funny how hard it can be some-times to convince other people that one is still alive.

Christine's Frustration

Driving back from some work I had in North Carolina, Vicky and I stopped overnight at a hotel. I dreamed that my daughter Christine was "frustrated". I don't remember any scenes of Christine in it, but only a feeling, and maybe seeing a heavy cloud representing this frustration, that was consuming her. I woke from the dream, and while lying in bed, I interceded for Christine breaking off that spirit and assignment of frustration. Later, that very morning as Vicky and I were continuing our drive home, we got a call on my cell phone from Christine. She asked, "Dad, can I talk to mom?" I handed the phone to Vicky, remembered the dream, and immediately wrote down the word "frustration" on a piece of paper. When Vicky was done I asked to talk to Christine. As Vicky handed me the phone, I handed Vicky the note. I asked Christine, "In the last twenty-four hours what has been the most dominant overriding emotion you have been experiencing?"

She responded, "Dad, I've just been so frustrated." She continued by saying how she had found out the previous day that her tailor hemmed her wedding dress too short at the bottom. I told Christine to repeat that sentence to Mom as I handed the phone back over to Vicky. Vicky listened to Christine tell her that she was so frustrated which was verification to her that I indeed had heard from the Lord in my dream earlier that morning. I took the phone back and told Christine I had an alert and warning from God this morning regarding her frustration. I then said that God knows her situation and revealed it to me to intercede; and He has the situation under control. The real problem and warning, I told her, was not the dress, but instead the frustration that had unseated the peace of Christ from ruling her heart and was now doing the ruling of her emotions and her actions. I explained that it is important to immediately give the situation over to God and reclaim that peace. The devil has been given place through the door of her frustration for possible evil to befall her. Christine understood, and we finished the phone call. She solved the hem problem, and I believe Christine was able to avoid any further disaster by making the proper adjustment in her emotions concerning the situation.

Casting Billy Out

Another "alert dream" story came to me from a young nineteen-year old woman who went to Christian school with my daughter. They were good friends. In her later years this woman explored the indie punk lifestyle. Christa started to be a part of a ministry that were known to be a part of that colorful lifestyle. We were watching a softball game when Christa came to say hello to us. She heard I was in dream ministry and when we got on the topic of dreams, she then told me of an experience she had.

She said she had a dream about one of her Goth friends. In the dream Christa was casting a demon named "Billy" out of her friend. She thought the dream was quite strange. Upon telling her friend about it, her friend sheepishly responded that she indeed had an "invisible friend" that she talked to and yes, the invisible friend's name … was "Billy"! I encouraged Christa that she was truly hearing from God and that upon further prayer she may find the action step to be, as in the dream, to go to her friend and cast Billy out of her. After all, it is our jealous God who wants to be our invisible living and true friend who lives inside of us. I told her she might want to seek the help of the Goth ministry since they were accustomed to do deliverance of this type.

CHAPTER 14

SEEING PEOPLE WE KNOW IN OUR DREAMS

Many times people will have a dream with a former high school or college classmate in it? Then upon waking they wonder why in the world that person they hadn't seen in years, was present in their dream? More than not, the dream is not about that person directly. The dream is usually speaking about what that person *represents* to the dreamer. He/she is merely a symbol of something that is present within the life of the dreamer.

The first thing we need to do with our dreams is view the objects in that dream symbolically. Ask, "What is the most significant thing about the person I dreamed about?" For example: If the most prominent thing or characteristic about the person was that he/she was an angry person, the dreamer should search his heart for where there is anger present. It probably won't take too long to find. The Lord may want to deal with this anger issue. He will generally show more about that issue in the rest of the dream. The level of success one has in interpreting dreams is directly related to the degree in which one is able to look at them symbolically.

There are times however that dreams are referring directly to the person or persons in the dreams. While the percentage of these types of dreams is very low, we need to excel in our interpretive skills and be able to discern the difference. This is a difficult process. There are a few ways to make these determinations. First, attempt to interpret what the person represents symbolically. God is not trying to make this difficult and interpretation usually comes with an earnest pursuit. Plug in what that person represents into the rest of the dream. If after thinking in this respect, and symbolism is not making any sense, there is a possibility that it may be about the person. There are other factors that could help determine this. Is the person the main star of the movie, so to speak? Does the dream center around him? Certainly, if anger is what God wants to address in one's heart, then this person may very well be the main actor in the dream. But again, if it just doesn't make sense, then ask the Lord if the dream is literally about this person.

I usually tried to find and contact the person I dreamed about the next day. During the course of regular conversation, I would simply ask how the person was doing. Depending upon my relationship and comfort level with the person, I might tell him that I have been observing and learning what my dreams may be saying to me. I sometimes then tell the person he was in a dream I had. I would tell the person the dream and would then ask if anything in the dream reflected anything going on in his life. I am considered to be a wild and crazy guy by many so people. They aren't surprised when I make a call to them with a dream. I also have "the dare" to do that. If we are sincerely interested in finding out the degree in which our dreams have revelation and truth, then we may need to step out of the box now and then. The results may be surprising. I was surprised. I found that many times the dreams did in fact reflect something going on in the other person's life. Many times the person has been greatly ministered to through my calling them.

Very little has been known about dreams that concern others. This is a delicate area. If we see a known person in a coffin in our dream, for instance, we don't want to call that one up and say, "Hey, I dreamed you were dead and in a coffin last night!" This would not be good. We must use caution and sensitivity while learning about dreaming of others. This is critical. Most people would discourage contacting a person who had been dreamed about. It is generally considered taboo to approach the person. Those who would caution in this area have our best interest in mind as well as the best interest for the body of Christ. That goes far in keeping order in the church and community. However, what if the dream indeed is about the other person with a need? The number one thing we need to do is to pray for them. At times the Lord may have the dreamer do more, but be sure to pray first and foremost. Then proceed with sensitivity and discernment.

We need to learn more about how to deal with these types of dreams. If these type of dreams occur only one percent of the time over one year, that could represent ten or more dreams in a year. I have found that these ten dreams, in the end, could be very life-changing or even-life saving to the one dreamed about. We need to learn to discern, interpret, and apply them appropriately.

Warning Dreams Concerning Our Loved Ones

I have discovered that most of these dreams concern loved ones or the dreamer himself. I have very few accounts of people having a warning dream of someone outside of their family or very close acquaintances. It does occur and can occur, but it is rare. It is a comfort to me to know that if the lives of my wife or one of my children is in danger, that the Lord would give me warning of that. It makes sense. I am a steward over my children, and I am one with my wife. Of course, if my own life is in danger the Lord can warn me through a dream of my own or through another member of my family. I have heard many stories of children receiving warnings concerning another family member. Isn't this enough reason to pay attention to our dreams? Too many have had the dream, suffered the loss of a loved one, but didn't know there was a need to respond. Too many have died prematurely. It grieves me to hear the stories of people who have lost loved ones; even more, when they have had the dream but didn't respond. We can change this. We can learn to respond to these dreams so that life is saved and sustained. The point of this book is this: Even if a person only receives one warning dream in his entire life, would it not be worth knowing how to respond appropriately in order for that loved one to be spared of tragedy or death? It would be worth it. It is worth it to God. He does not need our loved one in heaven more than we need him here on earth. I believe that long life is God's intent for us. We must be watchful to that end to do our part when called upon to do so. We have more to do with our loved one's safety than we think.

We certainly don't need a warning to pray for our spouse or children often and regularly. One day years ago, while musing on how much prayer is enough, the Lord spoke to me and said, "I love your wife and children more than you do. If there is ever a problem, I will let you know about it." I was a little stunned by that. I had to question if that was really the Lord speaking that in my heart? I asked myself can He really be trusted to that extent? That seemed foolish once I said it. Of course He can be trusted. The real question is will I be diligent to pay attention and be faithful to what I see or hear? That doesn't mean I can't and don't in general pray for my wife and children otherwise. It does mean that I don't have to live in fear wondering if I am praying enough. What a relief! Over the years my children have come to know that God speaks to Vicky and me in critical times in their lives. They live in confidence that we will be faithful to intercede according to those things we hear and see from our loving Father in heaven. Jesus said He only did and spoke that which He heard from His Father. Before dying He told his disciples in John 16:13, that the Holy Spirit, which was to come would, "not speak on His own *authority*, but whatever He hears He will speak; and He will tell you things to come." The Holy Spirit only speaks to us that which He hears from heaven. In the book of Acts Peter and John were commanded by the rulers and elders of Israel not to speak or teach in the name of Jesus again. Their response to them in Acts 4:30 was, *"... we cannot but speak the things which we have seen and heard."* We should be no different. We need to respond by doing, speaking, and even praying according to those things we see from the Father through our dreams, and the various other means He speaks to us. These are our most powerful prayers. These are the prayers that carry the most authority in our lives against all the schemes of the enemy.

CHAPTER 15

DREAMS OF OTHERS

Dreams of Loved Ones

The Lord will primarily send warning to those whose loved ones are about to come under attack by the enemy. This would particularly include one's spouse and children. My wife and I have had many warnings concerning our children. The warnings come to us mostly through warning dreams or angelic visitations in the night. I have not discussed angelic visitations of the night in this book, as I will be later writing a book exclusively about angels bringing warnings and alerts to us. Many may say they have never received a warning concerning a loved one. I don't remember ever having a warning about my children until I started diligently paying attention to, and recording my dreams. God has always given me warning concerning my loved ones, but I just wasn't paying attention or believing He would or could do such a thing. By not paying attention all the previous years, these many words from the Lord have just fallen to the ground. Since beginning to pay special attention to these ways the Lord communicates to us, I have increased in the degree in which I hear from the Lord. Each parent and spouse is missing many, many warnings over time as a result of not paying attention. There has been such a lack of knowledge and understanding of how critical dreams can be for a healthy and safe life. The results of this have been and are tragic. It is time to wake up in the Body of Christ and establish a doctrine of dreams.

Son Killed in Auto Accident

I went to visit a friend at a hospital a few months ago. Adjoined to this small community hospital is an Assisted Living Center. I knew a woman there who was an old friend of the family and decided to pay her a visit as well. On the way down the hallway to her room, I was talking to the daughter-in-law of the woman I had just visited in the hospital. The daughter-in-law walked with me to my next stop. She knew the woman as well and was going to assist me in finding the room. I had just told her that after all the years of hearing about people who had warnings prior to the premature death of their loved ones, it became a standard question to ask the dreamer, "Did you get the dream?" More than not the reply has been: "Yes! How did you know about the dream?" I told her that I would then proceed by ministering how our loving Creator gives us warning of such things that we might be able to avert the disaster. We came into the woman's room. She had other visitors including her husband and two other women friends. After some conversation the husband asked me, "Are you still doing that dream stuff?" I responded affirmatively.

One of the women broke into the conversation saying she had always wondered about one haunting dream in particular she had many years ago. I knew this woman and her history as I had grown up in the same small town. My mind quickly went to her youngest son, who years earlier, had been killed in an auto accident. I knew what she was about to say. She said, "About two months before my son, Jeff, was killed in the auto accident, I had a dream that he was indeed killed in a similar auto accident." I quickly explained to her that God had given her a warning dream. I explained that the church has little idea what these dreams are about nor how to respond effectively to them. I also ministered to her that it is not her fault. She never knew. We haven't had a doctrine in the church for dreams in general, much less warning dreams. She said that she had been living with a fear these past fifteen years since that accident that she would one day wake up from another such dream of her only remaining son being killed. How sad!

What a stealing of one's peace. All because we in the church haven't been able to understand or believe that God speaks to us out of love for us in order to save the lives of our loved ones. Oh, what other people must be going through who have experienced the same as this woman had. I was able to tell her what to do in case this type of dream ever happened again. I told her the prayer of faith is all that is needed. That she can pray with confidence in the name and power of Jesus Christ. Oh, so simple! So effective! She was now able to gain understanding, fifteen years later and with new knowledge to move on in her life, void of that old fear.

Granddaughter's Drowning Accident

I was staying at a couple's house while teaching at a two-day meeting in Iowa. The wife, Diane, told me her mother, who was a Christian, had a dream that Diane's daughter was in a car accident. She saw the car falling into water and saw the granddaughter drowning. She awoke and prayed. Soon after, the young woman *did* have a car accident where the car went into water. She was able to crawl out and lived.

My Dream of Christine Having Rabies

In 2005 I had a dream that my daughter Christine had rabies. I quickly realized that this is a warning dream. The dream played out in both a literal and symbolic way. It is too lengthy to explain in this book so I have made it available on my website instead. In addition to me receiving the warning in a dream, Vicky received an angelic visitation alerting her of imminent danger concerning Christine as well. It gives yet another example of how God is concerned about the lives of our children and gives us sufficient warning for us to respond and keep tragedy from coming.

Dreams of Other People You Know

Ephesians 6:13 Therefore take up the whole armor of God, that you may be able to withstand in the evil day, and having done all, to stand…18 praying always with all prayer and supplication in the Spirit, being watchful to this end with all perseverance and supplication for all the saints--

An old friend of mine, Todd, called me from his home in Texas one day. He had been my roommate for five years before I got married. He had moved away from Minnesota over twenty years earlier and had heard I was into dreams and interpretation. He told me he found it strange that in the last month he had dreamed three times about my aunt, Diane. My aunt had lived in the same town Todd and I had lived in. Todd rarely met her or even talked to her during that time. He explained that in all three dreams, he heard the Lord tell him that He was trying to get in touch with Diane. Todd asked me what that might mean. I responded, "It means the Lord is trying to get in touch with Diane, but for some reason Diane isn't directly getting the message the Lord is attempting to send her." So why would my friend from twenty years ago receive these dreams about my aunt? I don't know. There are many things we don't understand concerning God's ways. At least Todd was listening and was faithful in sharing the dream with me.

I knew I had a responsibility to pray that Diane would get the message the Lord was trying to send to her. Upon hanging up, I felt the Lord wanted me to immediately call her and alert her. I knew Diane was a Christian and believed she would be receptive to this. Diane had since moved away to Arizona, and I couldn't find her new phone number. Knowing my parents were wintering out in the Phoenix area, I picked up the phone to call and ask them for Diane's number. My father answered the phone and I asked him if he could give me Diane's number, as I needed to talk to her. He responded that Diane was presently standing right next to him and said I could talk to her right now. Diane and her husband lived about two hours away from my parents and had come to visit that day. Diane got on the phone, and I relayed the message to her. I told her the Lord was trying to get in touch with her. I encouraged her to seek Him diligently in the days ahead to receive the message he had for her. She accepted the word graciously, and we ended the conversation minutes later. What timing of the Lord. What were the odds that she would be at my parent's home the moment I called! God is a loving Father and indeed works in mysterious ways!

The Four-year Old Driver Dream

"I dreamed a four-year old boy, I knew, dangerously backed a tractor up and getting killed with four other people."

This woman instinctively prayed for the boy in light of her dream. The woman then followed up saying, "A week later, while the boy's mother was picking him up at daycare, he got into the car by himself and backed the car up across a busy street. His mother said it was a miracle he didn't hit anyone."

Giving a Man the Wrong Pills Dream

"I dreamed I gave a man who I knew a wrong pill and he died. A week later, I arrived at work and the caregiver I was replacing told me the same man in my dream was sleeping and hadn't been able to give him his medication. When he woke up I was suppose to give him the medication. I did as I was told and discovered later that the medication I had given the resident had been discontinued and should not have been given. Fortunately, it did not have an adverse affect on him."

Dreams of Strangers

Many of our warning dreams may involve disasters or death or harm to strangers. We would pray the same way we would for a loved one. All life is valuable and if God gives you such a dream you are responsible for responding faithfully. That stranger in your dream can, at times, represent a loved one and is no stranger at all. Take the following story for example.

Christine's Bull Goring Dream

I was visiting with my brother, Kent, in Fergus Falls, Minnesota one afternoon. I received a call on my cell phone from my daughter, Christine, in Seattle. She had just married Kaliber a year earlier and moved there as he and his family were from that area. They lived about 30 miles from his parents. Kennet and Jody Olson, Kaliber's parents, own a Black Angus farm on the outskirts of a Seattle suburb. Through our children's marriage we had become very good friends, and the whole family is passionate Christians. They all have quickly come to learn about dreams and warning dreams. They were witnesses to things the Lord had given Vicky and I over the first year of her marriage concerning Christine through dreams. They saw the fruit bearing of these dreams.

I have Christine on the phone in tears telling me that Kennet and Jody had been at a cattle auction. They were helping to herd a bull from one pen to another when this bull charged Jody, gored her, and threw her into the air. She had just been taken to the Emergency Room with apparent rib and knee injuries. I was saddened by the news and told Christine I would certainly be in prayer, I asked her to keep me posted. She then stopped me and said, "Dad, there's one more thing; I had the warning dream!"

I said, "What! Christine! Why didn't you pray against the assignment of the enemy? You know better!" She responded tearfully, "Dad, I didn't pray because in the dream it was a stranger who got gored. It wasn't anyone I knew!" I calmed down quickly and calmed her down. We had learned a valuable lesson at the expense of horrible injuries to Christine's mother-in-law. The accident caused Jody much pain, and she had to endure a long recovery process. Even if it is a stranger, we need to pray. It could be anyone.

Here is the dream my daughter sent me following the phone call.

Friday February 24th, five days before the bull attack. In the dream, Kennet and Jodi were going to sell their house. We were going through it to find things we needed to fix up for potential buyers that come and see it. I just remember going from room to room looking at what needed to be fixed. In Kris's room there were spider eggs on the ceiling that were being born. There were tiny spiders crawling out of the spider egg ball attached to the ceiling. We then were outside and it was nighttime. There was a huge fenced-in-area with dirt-ground instead of grass. More like a rodeo arena than fenced in area at a farm. There were lights and people gathered all around the fence as if there was going to be a show. There was one black bull in the arena. A girl [a stranger] stepped into the arena as if she was going to taunt it. She did and the bull charged her. She didn't get out of the way so it ran over her then preceded to ram its horns into her. What was suppose to be a fun show didn't turn out so fun.

Again, this was sent to me via email, after the disaster had occurred. My daughter knew the dream had warning signs: the bull attacking a girl and goring her; being dark outside may at times represent the presence of the power of darkness, the spider eggs on the ceiling showed that something eerie was being birthed in the lives of this family. Christine added later that Jody was in the dream watching the show only yards away from the girl who was gored. Christine said the show took place in what looked like the outside Kennet and Jody's house.

Many times there will be differences in dreams than what it is in real life. It was interesting that Christine was "going through it [the house] to find things they "needed to be fixed". This was a clue that there was something that she was in need of fixing through praying over this warning dream.

Not every element in a warning dream will be essential to interpreting the dream. We are looking for the gist of the dream. We are looking for the emotions of the dream feeling *so real!* Are we emotionally shaken by the dream either within it or when we wake up? Can the dream or parts of it be interpreted literally? In this case there were literally no spider eggs, not that I heard of anyway, but what the bull did in the pen was literally what happened, only not to a stranger. It was Christine's mother-in-law who was standing nearby.

Remember in my "Near Car Accident Dream"? I didn't know who was in those vehicles. It ended up being my three children and my son's band members.

The Red Car Over the Guardrail Dream

Here is another story of the lack of a response from someone who just didn't know how to recognize and respond to a warning dream. It comes to me via e-mail from Jackie who lives in Superior, Wisconsin. She attended monthly Hearing Group Meetings I facilitated in Superior over a couple of years' time. These meetings are formed as a result of teaching a dream class. They consist of those who want to go deeper and learn more about hearing God's voice.

Jackie's Email to Me

"… Amber, my daughter-in-law, had a dream last week Monday or Tuesday about a red car crashing through a guardrail and going into Lake Superior. It happened the next day in real life. An elderly man 88 years old, drove and broke through a guardrail by the deck in Duluth. His car was red and he died. The article was in the Duluth News Tribune Wednesday February 22nd, 2006 on the front page. Title of the article was: "Car Plunges into Harbor". I told Amber next time she has a dream to go into prayer right away. She is new at this stuff but extremely open. She did not receive any guilt as I told her it wasn't her fault and God wanted her to know how He is speaking in many ways."

Amber's Dream

The dream I had was between other dreams I had that night and was really short. It was just like a flash dream, I guess, of a red car driving over a guardrail. I thought it was strange because I was having one dream and then out of nowhere, I see a red car driving fast over a guardrail. I didn't think too much of it. I don't really know anyone that drives a red car, so I thought it maybe [didn't] mean anyone I knew. I didn't see any person. I was shocked when I read the paper a couple of days ago about the red car in the lake (Lake Superior). I guess God just wants me to keep praying.

Did you notice she said that the "flash dream" came out of nowhere interrupting the dream she was having? That's just like a "news flash" or an alert on television that breaks in on a television program. This came to her in what I call a "snapshot" type dream. Many times we get these quick snapshots either in a dream or a vision. Most of these are ignored because they come so fast. There is very little context to them. This is another hint alerting the dreamer that this is a warning dream. The Lord was simply showing this young woman that He needs our help and cooperation in bringing His life and saving grace to Earth. He is looking for ears to hear and faithful responders. What a tragedy that this man died needlessly and prematurely! One may say, "Well, Craig, he was 88 years old. It was probably just his time to go." I don't believe that. I can't believe that. If it was his time to go, then why did the Lord give Jackie's daughter-in-law the warning or revelation? No, this man had time left, and there was a war in the heavens over this man's life. God was shouting his warning from heaven for someone with ears to hear. Who else should have been paying attention in the days leading up to this old man's death? Let's wake up and be watching. We are called to the business of saving and sustaining lives in the name of Christ, both eternally, and from premature physical death.

Warning Ten Years Prior to Event

I was speaking at a home the day I was to have an evening meeting in the same city. It was a small group of people. After my talk on dreams, which always includes telling about warning dreams, an elderly man came up to talk to me alone. He started telling me a story about a dream he had about fifteen years ago. In the dream he was driving on a highway. Suddenly ahead of him was a situation that demanded quick thinking and maneuvering. He wasn't quite clear what the scene was but he made a decision to steer the car a certain direction which resulted in hitting a man and killing him. Then the man said that about ten years later he was driving down a highway and, lo and behold, there in real life was the same situation he had dreamed about. This man's dream immediately came to mind as he was now living the reality of it. But, because of the dream, he made a split second choice to steer the car in what would be considered an ill-advised direction. Because he did, the man he killed in the dream survived without incident. The reason I can't be more clearer in my description is because this man was weeping so heavily he was hard to understand. This man was so mystified and emotionally affected by the incident. What a powerful story! What a wonderful God! This man took the direction from the Lord and saved another man's life. Because of a dream, he knew he had to do the illogical if he were to avoid killing another man. The dreamer's life was spared as well. Well done, Sir!

I have learned that it doesn't matter who is in the dream. Whether we know the people or not, God is asking us to pray and intercede for others.

CHAPTER 16

MORE WARNING
DREAM STORIES

I have a small one-man business doing record preservation for county courthouses. From time to time I will have a larger job in which I rent a conference room in a hotel and hire temps from the city in which I am doing the work. In bringing up the subject of dreams and warning dreams to the temps, they have shared with me their stories.

House on Fire

One woman told of her father having a dream that their house was on fire, and burned it to the ground. It didn't look at all like the house they lived in. Years later, this Christian family moved to southern Missouri. One day the family's house caught fire and burned to the ground. Then the man remembered his dream and realized it was this house that he saw burning. It was the house he and his family would be living in, in the future. He didn't know he had the authority to pray it off at the time of the dream.

Fiery Auto Accident

Another woman in the same group told me that her husband was a meth user and even made the drug. One night, both she and her daughter had dreams that her husband and father respectively, died in a fiery automobile crash. The daughter told her mother all about the dream. Two weeks later the man was killed in a fiery automobile accident. He was hauling some type of oxygen or hydrogen tanks in the back of his pickup. Apparently they were needed in a meth lab. He went off the road, and the tanks exploded on impact. The entire truck was enflamed. They didn't know they could have prevented the death of their loved one by praying in Jesus' name.

Helicopter Crash

Another woman doing work for me in a different city told about how she had a dream that she saw a helicopter flying overhead. Suddenly, it flipped upside down and fell to the ground. A man whom she didn't recognize fell out of the helicopter and died.

When she woke up that morning, she took her children to daycare and went to work. On the way home from work that evening, she stopped to pick up her children. The daycare woman told her she had better come in and see something on the 5 o'clock news. The woman went in and sat down on a couch. The reporter told about a policeman who was also a pilot. The policeman had the day off and had rented one of these smaller gyrocopters and had taken it for a flight. There was a malfunction of some type, and the copter fell to the earth killing the man instantly. The man was this young woman's father. She was not a professed Christian, nor did she know that her dream was a warning from heaven. In the dream the man was a stranger. She didn't have knowledge of warning dreams or the power of prayer. She became a victim of her own dream. I believe she could have called out to God concerning this tragedy, and God would have intervened and saved her father's life. He is being totally faithful and loving to his creation. He is all about life, and He is doing what is necessary on His part to sustain it. We need to do our part. We need to believe!

Woman's Son Dies

I gave an all-day dream class in Davenport, Iowa, a few years ago. As always, towards the end of the class, I speak at length on God's warnings and alerts in our lives. As I was speaking an older woman announced that she had a dream years ago that her son died. Two or three days later, he in fact died. No further specifics were given as she sat and cried except to confirm what I was saying.

Korean War Casualty

While writing this chapter during a two week retreat in Arizona, I went to tell the neighbor across the street that I was renting the park home unit for two weeks to write a book regarding warning dreams. She was a Christian and nodded her head as I explained some of the stories to her. She then told me the story of her husband who early in their marriage, was fighting in the Korean War. One night she was awakened out of sleep and immediately sat up in bed. She sensed that something was wrong, and she knew it concerned her husband. She prayed for him and lit a candle asking God to put a light on his path. Two weeks later she received a letter in the mail from her husband telling her the story that coincided with the evening she was praying. Her husband and his commanding officer were crawling on their stomachs side by side. Heavy enemy fire broke out, and her husband's officer was killed, but her husband came out of it alive.

Virtually everywhere that I talk to people about warning dreams, someone comes forward and tells me a similar story. Many are grateful for the teaching and understanding they received concerning a loving God who gives a warning so that they might pray. It all made perfect sense to those who heard my take on it. They were at peace in knowing they weren't crazy, and it wasn't the devil giving the dreams. Of course, most of them lost loved ones as a result of not knowing how to respond. For that I am greatly saddened. As some small consolation I tell them it wasn't their fault. They didn't know they were supposed to pray and break off the enemy's scheme to come and bring death and destruction to their lives. The church never told them. The church hadn't known, either. I hope that will change.

The Tsunami Warning

On Saturday, Christmas Day 2004, I received a call from my friend, Pastor Moses who lives a few miles from the coast of India. I met this man while on a short-term missions trip in 1998. We have maintained our friendship over the years, and he had called to wish my family and me, "Merry Christmas."

I had been away that evening at relatives and returned to hear his message on the answering machine. The next day Sunday, December 26th, we heard the news about the tsunami that hit the coasts of Indonesia, Sri Lanka, Thailand and India. Immediately I realized that Andre Pradesh was one of the areas hit, as it lies on the coasts of the Bay of Bengal. Moses' home is just five minutes from the ocean. Three days later, we received another call from Moses. He gave a first hand account of the devastation and lives lost in his area. He reported at that time an estimated 13,000 people had died in India with 4,000 deaths alone from the region of Andre Pradesh where he lived. Being far enough away from the coastline, his family was alive and safe. He told how he had been conducting the church service. Upon finishing his message, he started receiving phone calls on his cell phone from people wondering if he was okay. He told them he had no knowledge of the disaster and later went to check out the devastation at the coast.

He was aware of my work and ministry in dreams and visions and had one month earlier asked if I could come back to India to teach approximately 100 Indian pastors about dreams and visions. Before hanging up, he said that he received a report from a pastor who formerly lived in the same city that Moses resided in. The Pastor had moved to Visage, India, another coastline city farther up the coast. One week before the tsunami this pastor had received a dream. In the dream God told him an earthquake was coming. This man then went to the church for the Sunday service and announced to the congregation the warning in the dream. The congregation prayed and interceded in response to the news from God. Moses stated that when the pastor called him, the city of Visage had reported that no one had died there from the results of that tsunami. That was miraculous because every community on the coastline was devastated by the tsunami. Deaths had been reported up and down that coastline. One man had heard and obeyed, and the church and their city were protected. Certainly, one could have interpreted the dream symbolically that a "spiritual tidal wave" or "quake" of revival is coming to this man's church or city. But this man of God felt it was literal that an earthquake was indeed coming, and the people responded in prayer. We must remember that there hadn't been a tsunami in that area in that man's lifetime. Most would not have believed that such a quake was about to happen. What faith!

On a Further Note Regarding the Tsunami of 2005

There were many reports that before the tsunami disaster hit, animals of all kinds, were heading inland to safety. Almost all of the animals survived compared to the thousands of people who died. Elephants carrying tourists fled for the hills just before the tsunami hit. There were stories of animals behaving strangely before the disaster. Scientists have studied this phenomenon wondering why animals can sense pending dangers and humans can't. Is it only the animals that have these extraordinary senses?

CHAPTER 17

FALSE WARNINGS

I have mentioned that not all dreams are God dreams. It is generally accepted that dreams come from one of three sources: God, the devil, or ourselves.

God Dreams

God Dreams have generally been defined and accepted as a dream directly sent by God. I would include it in the classification of one of the Outpourings of the Holy Spirit. These dreams are sent from heaven for our instruction, direction, encouragement, correction, warning, and revelation. I came to know my God dreams by the ones that were full of light. It has been accepted by many that a God dream is generally a dream that is in vivid color. Sometimes it could come as a black and white dream or in muted colors with one particular element in the dream in vivid color. While I agreed that our God dreams are our vivid color dreams, I couldn't justify that scripturally until I realized that things are in vivid color when there is a presence of a full or efficient amount of light. That made sense to me because in the scriptures it says, *"God is light"*. I have heard it said that it is impossible for a human to dream in color. Of course, Jesus said, in Matthew 19:26 *"… With men this is impossible, but with God all things are possible."*

Dreams From the Devil

Some believe that we also can receive dreams from the devil. Indeed there is probably not a dreamer who hasn't ever had what one would call a nightmare or night terror. I question whether the devil can, at will, give us dreams. I have never read in the Scriptures that the devil gave anyone a dream. I do believe, however, the devil can have influence into our dreams through our soul. We have excessive fears and anxieties in our life that I believe open the door to Satan to cause us to be horrified in our dreams. So indirectly, I see Satan's influence. I choose to say and believe that we have God dreams and soulish dreams. I don't find it worth arguing over; I just need to point out that there are a couple of thoughts on this. I certainly understand how demonic and horrifying some dreams can be. I just don't personally believe that we can receive a dream from the devil except through unredeemed areas of our soul.

Soulish Dreams

A soulish dream has generally been defined as a dream that comes out of our soul. It is generated as a result of our life in this world and things that we feed into our hearts. People sometimes ask me how often a person receives a dream from God. I reply that it generally depends on how much time they spend thinking on things that are from above versus things that are on this earth. The scripture says in Colossians 3:2, *"Set your mind on things above, not things on the earth."*

Early on in my dream ministry a man e-mailed me one day

claiming his fifteen-year-old son had incredible "spiritual warfare" dreams. He asked if I would take a look at some. This boy's father said that his son was a devout and zealous Christian. I told the father to have his son e-mail me three or four of his recent dreams, and I would take a look at them. Upon receiving them I was shocked and bewildered. Certainly these dreams were filled with flying beings that were at war with one another. Each dream was similar in that way. I showed them to my wife. We had not seen such dreams coming from an individual that had that sort of demonstration, at least not to this degree and in so many dreams. In seeking their meanings the Lord urged me to e-mail the young man with this question: Do you ever play those video war games? He e-mailed back that he did. It was his favorite pastime, and he did it on a regular basis. I then e-mailed him back saying that I would suggest he fast from playing those games for one month. Then I would be happy to interpret any dream he would have at the end of that time. I never heard from him again. This boy was filling his soul with a steady and heavy dose of those video games. Matthew 12:34 says, *"Out of the abundance of the heart the mouth speaks."* Similarly, out of the abundance of what we let into our soul, the soul dreams. Garbage in and garbage out.

When I first got into my county records preservation business about twelve years ago, I would take trips out of state. When I returned home, I had a desire to spend quality time with my young family. Surprisingly, I found most often time spent with each other was in front of the television. Soon, my wife and I made the decision to cancel the cable television. We didn't have an antenna on our house. Without cable we could not get even one channel to come in on our color television. Interestingly, after six months without television I asked my kids how they would feel if we got cable back. They all said, "NO! We don't want it back!" However, after a couple of years with no television, we have experimented with having cable back. After all, we were now empty nest, and it might be kind of nice having it. First, we found it so fun and intriguing that we probably watched more than we should have. Worse than that, my dream life turned incredibly more soulish. I would watch television before bed. With that being the last things that I dumped into my-self, my dreams reflected this. I had less and less God dreams per se, and I finally grew tired of it. I personally have a tendency to watch too much, and I don't seem able to have the self-control I should have. We constantly face decisions in our life on what we put into us. Yes, there are some healthy television shows. But anything done in extreme measures will affect one's dream life. Take heed what is heard and seen!

CHAPTER 18

ALERTS–GOD'S WARNINGS OF THINGS PRESENT

Reggie Jackson Hit by a Pitch

When I was in my early twenties I had a dream one night that I had a bird's-eye-view of the New York Yankee Reggie Jackson lying on home plate in agonizing pain. In the dream I imagined that a pitch, must have hit him while at bat. That morning I went to a local restaurant for breakfast. I purchased a newspaper from a machine. Opening up to the sports section, to my amazement, was a large photo of Reggie Jackson writhing in pain as he lay on home plate.

Sometimes we will receive warnings in our dreams of things that are already present in our lives or in the lives of others. I have termed these "Alerts". I include these with prophetic warning dreams because, like warnings of future things, the dreamer is not responding to these present warnings. These are critical. What was the purpose in the Lord showing me what had happened to Reggie Jackson the night before? I am not sure, but I know I could have prayed for him that he doesn't suffer anything worse from the injury. I do know that I have had many dreams that reveal things that don't seem to be too serious. I believe He gives them in order to show me that the He is able to bring me revelations of present and future realities. I call it good practice for some of the more serious times to come. There is so much knowledge God can give us; not only of present realities, but also things to come. Hebrews 2:1 Therefore we must give the more earnest heed to the things we have heard, lest we drift away.

"Pray For Me" Dream

My cousin Dana and I meet about once a week for coffee. One day he told me he had a dream that our cousin Bob came to him and said, "Pray for me." Dana thought that was strange, and I told him he should obey the word in the dream and be interceding for Bob. Dana, incidentally, is a disciplined intercessor who fasts often and intercedes for hours at a time. About four days later we received the news that our cousin Bob had testicular cancer and had gone into surgery that day. Would it have made some difference in Bob's outcome had Dana immediately heeded the call? Maybe Dana would have been prompted to contact Bob and tell him about the dream. We are not sure of Bob's relationship to Christ. What a witness and great encouragement it would have been for Bob to know that our loving Creator was looking out for him, spreading the word to those He knew could intercede for him. I can't say for sure, but as Christians we are called to answer the door when the Lord comes calling. Bob did survive his ordeal with cancer after successful surgery and recovery.

1Corinthians 1:27 But God has chosen the foolish things of the world to put to shame the wise…

Of course, many people aren't going to want to call up complete strangers or even some acquaintances or relatives in fear of being looked at as being crazy. This is something the Lord will lead each dreamer through. He will help to us. Ultimately, one may have to appear as a fool for Christ's sake in taking actions of obedience. The good news is that there is a connection and a confirmation on the other side of that which is heard from the Lord. Here is where simply trusting in the Lord is needed. In our presentation to others, we need to let them know that we are just learning in this area and are just trying to be faithful in our obedience to the dream and the Lord. Overall, I have felt great joy more than embarrassment through talking to those whom I have dreamed. This is what the Kingdom of God on earth is to look like. I want to encourage everyone that wonderful things happen when we step out with the things we hear and see. Mistakes will be made, but in Christ we are allowed that. We need to stop being so shy about this and press into the things the Lord would have his servants know and do. We live in a needy and dying world and, for many, one without hope. We are His ambassadors. We need to take courage and not be timid as the Lord grows us in this area.

The Spirit of Gary Dream

In the early years of learning to interpret dreams I had three dreams in two days concerning a church in our area of which I was not a member. I had visited the church from time to time over the years when they had various guest speakers come speak. That was the extent of my relations with that church.

In the first dream, I dreamed this pastor was giving me a tour of the church. We were in the basement. He brought me into a bathroom. It had definitely been cleaned up, and the walls had been painted. As we came in, we heard a sound coming from the cold air return vent high up within a wall to our left. We immediately both recognized it as being the sound of two people engaging in sexual intimacy. We knew the sound had carried down from a room on the second floor of the church building. As I glanced at the pastor who was facing the wall, I could see a frustrated look on his face, as if he had suspected something like this had been going on. Then, my former high school friend and classmate, Gary, walked into the basement bathroom. I started talking to Gary and asked him what he was doing here as I knew he lived in Des Moines, Iowa. Gary lowered his head and said, "I may not ever need to work now." I didn't understand what he meant but he repeated in a couple more times. Then I asked, "Gary, that wasn't you up there with that woman?" He just responded again with, "I may not even need to work now". I didn't understand what he meant.

A Jezebel Spirit in the Church

I was able to interpret this dream as a Jezebel, manipulative and controlling spirit that was operating in this pastor's church. The two other dreams regarding his church came the following night. I didn't understand much about those two dreams, but I thought it very strange that I would dream about a church that I didn't even attend. Why would the Lord show me this? I prayed about it off and on for approximately two months. Then, the Lord told me that he wanted me to go tell the pastor about these dreams and specifically tell the pastor the interpretation of the first dream. I tried to get out of this. I had never gone to anyone before with a dream I had about someone else; at least not a pastor. Furthermore, the Lord's instructions were that I was to tell the pastor that it was "the spirit of Gary that had come back to haunt his church." I really was freaked when I heard these instructions. I thought how foolish that would sound! What if that made no sense to the pastor? I didn't even understand that!

Somewhat reluctantly, I got a hold of the pastor on the phone and made an appointment to meet at a restaurant in his town in the next week. The day arrived, and after some initial chitchat, I told him that I had three dreams in two days about his church. I explained that in the last couple of years I had been studying dreams and had been learning how to interpret them with some success. I told him I had been told by the Lord to share these dreams with him. The pastor was receptive, and I began by telling him that based upon my first dream, there was a Jezebel spirit operating in his church. I said that the dream revealed that recently he had been suspicious about the existence of such a thing and ended by saying that this spirit existed in the first church that he pastored in the first years of his ministry. I then said that he would know what I meant when I say, "It is the spirit of Gary that has come back to haunt your church".

I then told him the last two dreams and said I hadn't been able to interpret what they meant. His response to all this was that he understood some of the things I said and didn't understand other things. The meeting ended shortly afterward without him responding any further. He thanked me for taking the time to share with him, and that was it. I felt terrible! I wished he had said more, for my sake, as I was feeling pretty embarrassed. I thought about what I had just said and done. Keep in mind; this was a first for me going to a pastor with a dream. I went home having only the satisfaction of obeying the Lord to the best of what I perceived Him to be telling me. I was just the messenger and needed to just move on believing I did what the Lord wanted me to do.

Confirmation of Interpretation

About ten days went by. I received a phone call one afternoon. It was this pastor's wife. She invited my wife and me to their home for the evening. We arrived early the next evening. After a good time of fellowship, the wife asked me if I would repeat the dreams and the interpretation that I had told her husband. Upon finishing she exclaimed, "You don't know what you are saying!" I had figured as much. The pastor spoke up and told us that within a week after our meeting, two prophets came to their church for a weekend conference. Both these men came up to the pastor and told him that they sensed a "Jezebel spirit" in operation in the church. In addition, a friend from many states away had called during the past week to tell them that he had been revealed the same thing. What a relief to hear of the confirmations. This dream had warned the pastor about an existing problem, which was confirmed three more times within the next two weeks. In addition, the pastor's wife confirmed that they had a Jezebel spirit indeed operating in their first call at a church in another community many years earlier. She explained there was a man in the church who would go around the community saying terrible things about them and the church. He had brought much destruction and agony to their ministry. That man's name was … Gary. Incidentally, my high school friend Gary had nothing to do with the situation of this church at all. The Lord just used him to give me the name of the person the pastor and his wife knew as a Jezebel.

I asked what this man did for a living. I was curious why my friend in the dream kept repeating the words, "I may not even need to work now". She replied that the man had suffered some sort of career ending injury and never worked again. Amazing!

This couple expressed their gratitude to me for sharing the dream and interpretation with them. This dream illustrates how the Lord gave warning to a ministry through a vessel that was simply willing to pay attention to his dreams and what the Lord was saying. Then, following through in obedience to what the Lord wanted me to do. At times we will feel like a fool for God. It brings great and critically needed revelation and help to a problem in a church. I trust God that it gave the pastor further revelation in dealing with this problem. In the end it also greatly strengthened my faith that the Lord speaks in mysterious ways. He wants to use us in these ways for His will and Kingdom to be advanced in this world. Am I telling everyone to go out and tell their pastor all your church dreams? Emphatically, *no*! We need first to learn much about the way God speaks to us in the dream world. We can work with others in the body in order to learn and grow in this area. We are looking to build up and not tear down. With time and experience these things will be made clearer. We need understanding from each other so that we can begin this process, over time becoming better and better at discerning God's voice through these types of dreams.

CHAPTER 19

THE HIGH SCHOOL SHOOTING

The following story is lengthy. It demonstrates how mysteriously and wonderfully God is able to give warning to a community of believers leading up to a crisis. It is a picture of how the church might one day function in responding to warnings from heaven once a doctrine of dreams is established.

Vicky and My Two Dreams

At 7:15 a.m. on the morning of Wednesday, September 24th 2003, I needed to drive my wife to school because we were short a vehicle. During the drive, my wife shared a dream with me that involved our son being stung by two bees at his school. He fled the school and ran into some nearby woods. As I dropped her off, she said we needed to pray for him and his protection for the day. He was a junior at St. Cloud Technical High School here in St. Cloud, Minnesota. As I drove off, I prayed for Paul and mused about a dream I had in the night about a principal at a school who was directing us to move furniture out of the school.

Do Dates in a Dream Mean Anything?

At 10:00 a.m. I returned a call to friends of mine. I had just returned the night before from being out of state for a week. They invited me out to their house for coffee and conversation. I arrived at about 10:20 a.m. and we sat in the dining room in conversation. At about 11:15 the husband got up from the table to answer the phone. His wife looked across the table and asked me if dates meant anything in dreams. I responded affirmatively that they indeed have meaning and could be very significant. I asked her why she wanted to know. She told me she had a dream with a date in it. I encouraged her to tell me the whole of the dream in order to possibly give her some insight interpretively. She shared the dream as follows:

The Bald-Headed Man Dream

On or about September 9th (approximately two weeks earlier) I had this dream. In my dream, I was in a long room, perhaps an apartment. The room appeared to be a living room. The room that I was in had walls that were very, very tall. They were painted a very pale blue. I was seated on a long sofa when all of a sudden a large, bald man with a moustache came bursting through the door carrying a boy. The boy had some type of leg injury. I did not see the face of the boy. The face of the bald man looked like our former Governor of Minnesota, Jesse Ventura. The bald man told me I had to take the boy to a doctor's appointment. He handed me a piece of paper with the appointments typed on it. The first appointment was sometime in July. I believe it was the 19th. I told the bald man that the first date was now past. Then he told me about the second appointment. I looked down at the bottom of the paper and saw the date "September 24, 2003". Then I woke up.

She ended the dream by saying, "Craig, today is September 24th!" I quickly overviewed the dream in my mind and glanced at the clock, which to my recollection said approximately between 11:15 and 11:20 a.m. I then said, "We need to pray *right now!*" We bowed our heads there at the table, and I prayed for whoever the boy was and whatever he represented. We didn't understand exactly, but asked God to come and help concerning the event revealed by the dream that concerned this day. I continued to pray that God would bring healing, deliverance, and help in whatever the dream represented. I prayed that through our prayers the harm or hurt would be minimized or prevented.

When finished, I explained that I believed the dream she had was a warning dream from God. I encouraged her to further pray for the event that was revealed through the dream, as the Lord would lead her. I explained this was common practice in our family when we get dreams of this type. I explained my conviction that God gives us these dreams so that we can intervene and through prayer change or avert the outcome of the event the dream speaks of.

The News Report of a School Shooting

I left the couple's residence at about 12:15. I picked up my daughter and took her out to lunch. When we finished, I went to the counter to pay. The hostess asked me if I had heard about the shooting that just occurred at Rocori High School in Cold Spring, Minnesota only ten miles away. I responded, "No." The hostess told us we could see the report on television in the adjacent bar area. We went to the bar and learned on the television that two high school boys had been shot by another boy classmate and rushed to the hospital in nearby St. Cloud. The television screen then displayed a picture of the gym teacher who stopped and apprehended the boy with the gun, thus avoiding any further casualties. My mouth dropped! He was a bald-headed man with a mustache who somewhat resembled Governor Jesse Ventura. Immediately, I was reminded about the woman's dream and knew this was to what her dream was referring. I also learned that the shootings occurred at around 11:35 a.m., or approximately fifteen minutes after the woman and I had prayed.

As my daughter and I got into my vehicle, I dialed the number of the dreamer and her husband. They were just going to call me. They had been listening to the Special Television Report, and I reminded the woman of the dream she had. She was already thinking about that. I told her to write the dream down immediately, for the record, just as she had told it to me earlier in the day.

Later that day, on another television report, I learned more about the tragedy at the school. The gym teacher was a former college football player from The University of Minnesota in Duluth. The suspect of the shooting was a freshman at the school. He shot one boy near the entrance to the gym and then ran into the gym and shot a second boy. He then turned and aimed the gun at the gym teacher who was sitting in the bleachers only feet away. The teacher immediately put his hand up in the air and hollered, "Stop!" The boy then dropped the gun and was then apprehended by that teacher.

Carey's 9:11 Alert

In mid afternoon I picked up my older son, Carey, from his college classes. Driving home, I told him about the tragedy. As I was telling him about the woman's dream, his eyes got wide and said, "Oh, no!" I asked what was wrong. He shared with me what happened to him that morning as his alarm woke him. He explained he was too tired to get up, and he decided to skip his first class. He reset the clock and fell back to sleep. He was awakened an hour later when the alarm again went off. He looked at the alarm clock that said "9:11". He interpreted this as an alarm going off revealing "911" an apparent emergency. He knew from similar incidents and previous dreams, including the September 11th one, that this was another warning from God. He felt the urgency and was moved to pray right there, not knowing what exactly the warning was about. He told me he prayed throughout the morning walking to school and during his classes.

Students Being Warned Through Dreams

At 5:30 p.m. that same day, a friend of mine came to our front door. I hadn't seen this man for months and I welcomed him in. As he walked in I realized that he lived only miles from Cold Spring. I brought up the shooting, and he replied that was why he had come to see me. He sat down and told me his son, Matthew, was in school this morning at Rocori High School. Matthew was in the same gym class in which the shooting had taken place. The father relayed to me what happened to Matthew and told me of some dreams that related to the shootings. Later, I received Matthew's story of what happened first hand in Matthew's own words:

Matthew's Story

Here is my story of the morning of the shooting, starting with my gym class: I went downstairs to my gym locker. My key to my lock was missing. I looked around for it, and thought that I might have left it in the band room where I kept my jacket. I proceeded to go upstairs to the band room. My key wasn't there either. Due to the delay, I resolved that I would not be participating in gym class that day. I made my way back to the gym to tell my gym teacher what happened. I was at the threshold of the gym door when I heard a shot ring out. I looked into the gymnasium and saw a boy with a gun shooting another boy execution style. The gym teacher, sitting in the bleachers, then stood up, put his hand up, and said, "STOP!" The boy was pointing the gun at him. At that time, I made my way downstairs to the boys' locker room. I was in shock. I had never felt like this before or after. It was like a bad dream with a buzzing sound and a slow motion type feeling that you see in movies. I grabbed a couple of people on my down the stairs and told them not to go upstairs because someone had a gun. I couldn't believe what I was saying. Two of the three people didn't even believe me, and went up the stairs anyway. I reached the bottom of the stairs. I looked to my left. Far down the hall I saw someone lying on the ground.

Two Dreams The Night Before The Shooting

Matthew then shared that his brother and Matthew's girlfriend each had a dream the very night before the high school shooting.

"My brother had a dream that he was in the kitchen and my sister came in and started shooting him. My girlfriend had a dream that I was shot in school by a boy." He added that his girlfriend was hysterical when she heard about the shooting. She remembered the dream and feared Matthew was dead.

Matthew's Dream About Five to Six Years Earlier

Matthew also was reminded that day about a dream he had five to six years earlier:

I had a dream about a boy at school. I was in a hallway and he had pointed a gun to my head and said, "Do you believe in Jesus?" There was a large shooting rampage. That's all that I remember about the dream.

Matthew added that the dream stuck with him because of its eeriness. He honestly believed in the back of his mind that one day he would see a large shooting. When Matthew was in seventh or eighth grade, a woman came to speak at the school he attended. She was a sister of a girl who was shot in the Denver Colorado Columbine school tragedy. While she spoke, Matthew was reminded of his dream. He had an eerie and gross feeling for the remainder of the young woman's presentation. He recalled that he then told someone about the dream.

Another Boy Killed the Same Day in Minnesota

The morning after the Rocori tragedy, I was reading the Minneapolis Tribune newspaper about the shooting. I happened to notice another article that told about another shooting and death of a boy in Duluth, Minnesota the same day as the Rocori shooting. A five-year-old boy was shot and killed when a couple of people tried to break into the apartment where this boy lived. The incident happened at 4:03 a.m. The boy and his two brothers had been sleeping on the fold-out-couch in the living room of the apartment. A man who was staying there with the boy's mother had tried to hold the door shut so people could not break in. It was suspected that this was a drug related incident. A gun was then fired through a crack in the door. A bullet hit the boy in the head. The boy died in the arms of his mother as the police arrived.

A Wake Up Call in the Night

A day after the shooting I went to minister at a Hearing Group Meeting in town. A Hearing Group is a group of people who gather in a home mostly for the purpose of learning more about dreams and how to interpret and respond to them. I held monthly Hearing Group Meetings in various communities in Minnesota and Wisconsin for a number of years. My teaching included warning dreams, alerts, signs and wonders. I taught people, at length, how to further recognize warnings, interpret them, and respond immediately to them to avert or minimize any pending disaster that the Lord may be revealing.

We talked at length that night about the shooting. I told them about all the warnings there had been. One woman then related the warning she received the night before the shootings. She said upon retiring for the night, she forgot to set her "thirty minute" timer for her television to shut off. She fell asleep with the television still on. Later in the night she was abruptly awakened by the sound of pounding on a door and the shouting of policemen saying, "It's the police! Wake up and let us in!" She sat up and found the commotion coming from a movie on her television. Based upon what I had taught, she took this as a sign from God alerting her that something was wrong and needed immediate attention. She got up and walked around the living room interceding for this "emergency feeling' the television scene gave her, until she felt released to go back to bed. She mentioned the main thing that came to her mind while praying was protection for her nieces and nephews. When she felt the release, she went back to bed. When she heard the news of the shooting the next day, she felt that was what God had alerted her to the night before.

Initial Interpretation of the Bald-Headed Man Dream

In my initial interpretation of the woman's Bald-Headed Man Dream, I saw that the Governor Jesse Ventura looking man represented authority. Jesse Ventura held the highest position of authority, politically speaking, in the state of Minnesota at that time. He represented the highest "spiritual" authority in the state of Minnesota, which of course would be God. To further confirm and strengthen this interpretation, the man represented Jesus by the first name of the Governor; "Jesse". The man bursting through the door represented a visitation from Christ to this woman through her dream. The abruptness of him coming through the door was the hint that there was an abrupt message or alert that needed immediate attention. The injured boy meant that there was a pending attack on a boy or boys. This dreamer was being given some instructions to get this boy to the Great Physician, Jesus, through the means of intercessory prayer. When the dreamer related to me that, "the first date was now past" I realized that in real life this woman had sat on the dream through lack of understanding without responding for weeks. In real life we may be too late in helping with one of the appointments for prayer. Realizing that we had already lost over eleven hours of the day, time was of the essence, and we needed to pray without any further delay.

Looking Back on the Dream

Once I found out about the incident, I was able to get the details. I then was able to look back and further interpret what the woman's dream was revealing.

"In my dream, I was in a long room, perhaps an apartment. The room appeared to be a living room. The room that I was in had walls that were very, very tall. They were painted a very pale blue. I was seated on a long sofa when all of a sudden a large, bald man with a moustache came bursting through the door carrying a boy…"

I realized that the woman who had the dream of the bald headed man actually had been warned of both the incident at the school and the incident in the Duluth apartment. In the same dream:

"I was in a long room," similar to a gymnasium "perhaps an apartment." Similarly the Duluth murder took place in an apartment.

"The room appeared to be a living room." The Duluth murder took place in the living room of the apartment.

"The room that I was in had walls that were very, very tall. They were painted a very pale blue." The gymnasium where the school shooting occurred of course had very, very tall walls; certainly not typical of an apartment. Unfortunately, I was never able to find out what color the walls were in the Duluth apartment living room nor in the gymnasium. I would guess one of the locations would reveal what the pale blue meant.

"I was seated on a long sofa." So were the three boys sleeping on a sofa bed. *"when all of a sudden a large, bald man with a moustache came bursting through the door."* Ironically, the murderer in Duluth was trying to also burst through the door of the apartment. *"carrying a boy. The boy had some type of leg injury. I did not see the face of the boy."* This revealed that the intended victim in general would be a boy. I never found out if any of the boys who died suffered any sort of leg injuries. The fact that she could not see the boy's face may reveal that it is not anyone that the dreamer knew. *"The face of the bald man looked like our former Governor Jesse Ventura. The bald man told me I had to take the boy to a doctor's appointment."* Again, this refers to the highest spiritual authority in Christ Jesus. The instructions to take the boy to a doctor appointment meant to take this to God in prayer with authority in the name of Jesus. The dreamer was now given authority, through revelation in the dream to break off this appointment/assignment of the enemy. It is also noteworthy that the man in the mustache looked so similar to the gym teacher who was sitting in the bleachers waiting for class to begin. The boy shot two boys and then turned and aimed the gun

at the teacher. The teacher "arrested" if you will, the shooter, by extending his hand toward the boy and shouting *"No!"* which caused the boy to drop the gun. The highest "authority" was in his firm voice, stopping the boy from committing any further violence.

"He handed me a piece of paper with the appointments listed. The first appointment was sometime in July. I believe it was the 19th. I told the bald man that the first date was now past."

This to me confirmed that the first appointment was concerning prayer for the Duluth boy. We missed the opportunity because she relayed the dream to me hours *after* the boy in Duluth was murdered. The incident in Duluth reportedly happened at 4:03 a.m. Could it be that July 19th could have meant the time of "seven hours and nineteen minutes"? Or more specifically, did the dream itself prophesy that, in real life, we would be seven hours and nineteen minutes late to pray for the boy in Duluth? From what I remember observing on the clock at the couples house, it was between 11:15 and 11:20. When she told me the dream, we immediately prayed. Seven hours and nineteen minutes after 4:03 a.m. would be 11:21a.m.

"Then he told me about the second appointment. I looked down at the bottom of the paper and saw the date "September 24, 2003". Then I woke up."

The second appointment represented the high school shooting assignment of the enemy God was revealing to the dreamer. We DID have time to pray off that assignment! We had less than fifteen to twenty minutes to pray, but we did make that appointment and followed the instruction in time. Unfortunately, we, and whoever else heard were not able to completely break off the assignment of the enemy on that day. We were able to minimize what happened, at least in the school incident.

Matthew's Life Spared

I believe in Matthew case, that Matthew was diverted from getting to the gym class on time due to intercessory prayer. I believe it was the plan of the enemy for Matthew to die that day. His girlfriend's dream would confirm my belief. She dreamed the night before the shooting incident that Matthew was *"shot in school by a boy."* Matthew himself had the dream years earlier of *"a large shooting rampage"* where a boy *"pointed a gun"* to his head. This again, revealed the intent of the powers of darkness for the son to be shot and killed. I believe Matthew's life was spared by reason of those who heard the warning and interceded. Unfortunately, I believe most of those who were warned, had no idea what to do with what they heard or saw in their dreams, or however else God sent the warning. That was certainly the case with Matthew's brother and girlfriend as well as Matthew's own dream. Matthew told me that, the day before the shootings, his best friend had been goofing around with Matthew's keys. Matthew believes that somehow, the key to his locker, fell off his key chain. He believes, had he not went back to the band room to look for his key, he would have been shot. He believes he would have been in the path of the shooter at the time of the rampage.

A Further Mystery

It's noteworthy to mention that the name of the five-year old boy from Duluth was Marcus Johnson. The hero at the high school shooting was Mark Johnson. The media reported the gym teacher went to college and played football at the University of Minnesota in Duluth many years earlier. What that is significant of, I don't exactly know. It was just a further tie-in for the two incidents that day on September 24th of 2003.

Warnings and incidents like these happened in Biblical times when God would give a person a dream or an angel visitation announcing upcoming calamity. Joseph was warned by an angel in a dream to take Mary and the baby Jesus into Egypt for a time while Herod ordered all male children up to two years old, in Israel, to be killed. Unfortunately, this woman did not interpret the dream and take the proper steps of instruction in interceding for these upcoming incidents. Because of asking about the date of September 24th and sharing the dream with me, at least we were able to do our part to help avert or minimize the assignment of the enemy at the high school even though it was last minute. Unfortunately, the boy and his girlfriend didn't take the proper action steps from their dreams to do their part to intercede in prayer either. They had no idea God worked that way. Very few people do. My wife's dream, my son's signal from the "9:11 alarm" clock, and the woman awakened by the authorities on the television all were promptings to pray against an impending assignment that occurred within hours of the warnings. Intercession was made as a result of those three warnings. Days after the 24th, a few more people told me they had warnings of the high school shootings as well. They failed to interpret the dream enough to see it as a warning and didn't pray.

In Summary

God reveals things through our dreams, including warnings of things to come. I have been alerted with these types of dreams many times over the years. I have spent time in prayer believing that my prayers have the power to avert or minimize events that would bring harm, destruction, or catastrophe. I further believe that God gives us warnings more often than we would think. If we would but pay attention to our dreams, and if we could interpret their meanings adequately, many of these disasters would be averted or minimized. As Jesus points out in the Parable of the Lampstand in Mark 4:24, we need to *"Take heed what we hear!"* That means we need to learn how to pay attention and respond appropriately to the things the Lord is saying in the earth. I believe many more people were given similar warning dreams prior to September 24th regarding the Rocori shootings and the Duluth shooting. Unfortunately, very few pay attention and understand their dreams, so they couldn't respond and do their part in prayer. We only know in part, and I believe that we have a loving Creator who gives every warning. It is my firm belief that there were enough warnings given from heaven that, if all of them would have resulted in prayer, these two tragic incidents on September 24th could have been totally averted and no lives lost as a result.

CHAPTER 20

WHY DIDN'T I GET THE DREAM

The warning dreams I have mentioned in this book are just a few of many that I have had or that others have told me about. Whenever I bring up the subject of warnings in my teaching, it is uncanny how often people will give me their story on a warning that happened to them or someone they know. This can't be coincidence. This is way beyond the realm of chance. Something is going on here. These are warning dreams just like in the Bible, only we haven't handled them correctly. We don't have a doctrine for dreams in the church, and we need one badly. We are without understanding as humans and need knowledge as to how to respond to such occurrences.

It is my intent that people, who read this book, hear me speak concerning warnings from heaven, or who have had these occurrences in their own life will contact me at my website and submit their testimony. I already have countless testimonies. I have, as they say, forgotten more than I have remembered or recorded.

I will also be listing the warning dreams that were too lengthy to include in this book. By this I hope to convince everyone everywhere that this is real. My hope is that one day, the knowledge and belief in warning dreams will be common.

I Am Sorry if you Have Lost a Loved One

As much as I have given evidence of God giving warnings today, I must say that there is even more we don't know and understand about these types of dreams. If you had the warning dream and indeed lost a friend or loved one soon after, I want to say I am sincerely sorry for your loss. I am grieved for all those who experienced this and didn't know what to do. I have heard too many stories of loved ones dying. It has deeply saddened me. It has led me to write this book. I want it all to stop. I also want to repeat what I told the woman whose son died in Lake Superior just weeks after she had "the dream". It is not your fault! You didn't know! None of us have known exactly how to respond. Most have never told anyone of this experience. Many told others and were told the dream came from the devil. I am sorry for those who have been haunted by this experience. The church hasn't known about nor learned to recognize this phenomenon and respond correctly and efficiently. I ask that you don't blame yourself any longer, but learn and be ready for the next alert or warning. We can change the outcomes of our future and the future of those we love; death shouldn't come prematurely.

Why Didn't I Receive the Warning?

This is a question that needs to be addressed. There are things I don't fully know or understand concerning warning dreams. I don't have all the answers. The biggest question that people will have is why didn't God give *me* a warning dream regarding the death of *my* loved one? I can address some of the reasons one may miss the warning.

The Warning Didn't Come In a Dream

Firstly, there is the possibility that the warning came by some other means than a dream. These warnings can come in the many various ways in which God reveals Himself. He could send it in a vision or by some other sign or wonder. I have testimonies of people receiving warnings through "that gut feeling." Others have simply awakened in the middle of the night with an overwhelming thought or feeling of impending danger. There can be many diverse ways the Lord could be attempting to reveal to us and we need to learn how to identify these ways. My next book in this series is called Angelic Visitations. This book will reveal how angels are present in our lives or sent to alert us of danger of things present as well as things to come. It is my hope that the readers of this book will give numerous testimonies of the diverse ways they have been warned.

The Warning Came to Someone Else

Secondly, maybe the warning wasn't given to you. Maybe it was given to another loved one. My conviction is God will indeed give warning whenever there is an assignment from the enemy to bring harm or death. I don't know how many people are intended to get the warning. I don't know if God will warn everyone or just enough people to deal effectively with the situation. Most of the time, one person is all that is needed. Which person receives that and why others don't remains a mystery and therefore is difficult to answer. One would think that, of course, a spouse would be warned about the other spouse, or the parent about their child. This could only be better learned by further study of case after case.

The Person Doesn't Remember His/Her Dreams

Many people don't remember their dreams. When I teach a class on dreams, I generally begin by asking how many in the audience dream. I have found that in a marriage at least one person is the dreamer. The husband might say, "I don't dream, but my wife dreams like crazy!" or vice versa. This is a good sign. As stated earlier, we all dream between three to seven dreams each night. The problem is that we haven't believed in the importance of dreams over time and therefore have not paid attention to them. It is vital that we learn to "sleep with our eyes open". We so need to pay more attention. As a society, we have discarded our dreams. We need to regain our belief in them; they are a way that God speaks to us from heaven. We need to repent for not paying attention and giving heed to them. We need listen to the dreams of our children. We can get these dreams back. We can ask God to help us remember those dreams from heaven. We generally have less than ten minutes before we forget most dreams. We need to learn to write down our dreams; especially the ones that invoke some emotion or carry some weight. Literal dreams don't need much interpretation and are the ones in which we can more easily understand. We can error of the side of caution. Over time you will begin to get a better grasp on these mysteries. I would suggest that one's last prayer before falling asleep each night to be, "Lord, if you have a dream for me this night, help me to remember it." There are more tips on remembering dreams, but the best one is that as soon as you wake up from sleep, whether it is in the middle of the night or the morning, ask yourself if you had a dream and write any of them down immediately. It only takes a few minutes before these dreams will be erased from your memory. This takes discipline and diligence. It will be worth it. Journaling your dreams is one of the most profitable things you can do in your life.

The Inability to Correctly Interpret the Dream

Most warning dreams can be interpreted quite literally. Still others can be quite symbolic. Very few people know how to interpret their dreams. This takes training and time. God is the revealer of these mysteries, and He needs to be sought after for interpretation. Sometimes the novice is able to understand his own dream, but most times we have little or no idea of the meaning. It is never too late to buy a book or take a class. Buying this book may be a beginning or continuing education. Don't stop learning. Most of all, ask the Lord for the interpretation. The Body of Christ has a lot of catching up to do regarding dreams. We can grow in leaps and bounds if we set our heart to do so.

Will God Give a Warning Every Time?

This is the million-dollar question. I don't know conclusively. I have stated before in Amos 3:7, "Surely the Lord GOD does nothing, Unless He [first] reveals His secret to His servants the prophets." This is true for today. Of course we each don't receive everything he is saying from heaven. We each "know in part" as the Scripture says. I have come to believe though, that we will be given the things pertaining to life concerning those we love and over whom are stewards. I also have come to believe that God has created and intended us to live long on the earth. There are two forces that can affect this great intention. Firstly, we know that Satan will endeavor to bring harm or death to us as he finds an opportune time. I don't know what actually warrants an attack, and why he comes when he does. I do know that we need to be alerted and prepared if and when he is about to come. We would do well to get the word ahead of time.

Secondly, I do know that as humans we reap what we sow. If one persists in unhealthy behavior one will ultimately reap the consequences of that behavior. If an alcoholic who gets intoxicated repeatedly drives 90 miles around a curve in the road and has a fatal accident, will we get a warning from heaven? Will God not give a warning when Satan is not the source or cause of such an accident? Is it our own doing that can bring harm or death to us without it being an attack from the enemy? Will God leave us to our own devices? Are we outside of his grace and love in this realm? Maybe God can't interfere in these cases. Maybe this principle of reaping what we sow exempts us from His warnings. We do know that He has given us our own freewill. Do we then conclude that God only warns us when it is coming from an external force and will outside of our own? These are all questions that we need to ask. I cannot conclude definitively that God will warn us in cases where we reap what we sow. Can the Devil be the cause of some accidents and not be the cause of others? I just don't know for sure. There maybe will be no warning in the cases of reaping and sowing.

What if It is Simply a Person's "Time to Go"?

Here again, I have changed my thoughts on this over the years of analyzing dreams. Christ came to give us life and life more abundantly. I have a hard time believing that God chooses some to die young and others to die when they are much older. I may be wrong, but I tend to believe now that forces of darkness try to keep us from having long and quality lives. Our own carelessness and reaping what we sow may also cut these times prematurely. It would seem strange to me that our Creator comes to give us life, and at the same time He wills for some a premature death. One could say that, "He is God. He can do whatever He wants to do." I understand that line of thought, but I wonder if he can counter who He has defined Himself to be and what He has proclaimed to be the truth. He won't break His own rules. I am left to believe from my experience with His warnings, that He desires us for long life. So then, when a person comes to a ripe old age, and their bodies have run the course of time, there is a time that God appoints for a day of death. In those cases, maybe there is no warning. This is God's will then to bring the end. I have accounts of many people who have dreams that reveal something is final about their elderly loved ones' life and are alerted to their coming deaths. These dreams are for the most part peaceful and sometimes emotional for the dreamer. This may be a way to help prepare people for their loved ones' departure.

What I Do Know

Through all the many stories of warning dreams that I have heard throughout the years, I am firmly convinced that lives would have been spared of death, disease, or injury had these dreamers known what to do with them. The best medicine is preventative medicine. It is easier to do what is necessary before a disaster than have to deal with it after the tragedy occurs. God's perfect will is for us to heed the call through His warnings. It is not His perfect will for us to ignore Him and His protection and deliverance from harm. It God's will for us to receive the antidote to the enemies plans against us. We don't want to have to deal with the results of not hearing and not heeding His warnings. It is very hard to understand how to pray and what to pray for when we have missed the perfect will of God. It only adds to our questions as to why a loved one isn't healed after persistent prayers for them. I believe we can have better. We do have something better. We can live in Christ in a much more powerful way by coming into the knowledge of His will and responding before, rather than after, a crisis occurs. Most of the time, Christians are praying after it is much too late. We need to hear the Holy Spirit telling us things to come. We need to learn how to interpret these things He tells us. We can be more valiant warriors through our prayers. We can experience mightier victories by taking authority and thwarting the enemy. We can grow in this grace. We have much to learn. We need to walk in the things that the Lord has destined for us, not what the Devil has destined. Lord, give us ears to hear and eyes to see, the things to come that the Holy Spirit is revealing.

Have You Had a Warning Dream from God?

If you have had a warning in the way of a dream, I would like to hear your story. If you have, it is my hope that yours had a fruitful ending. Unfortunately, most don't. Most people don't know they have the power and authority to break these foretold assignments of the enemy. I am looking forward to thousands of stories from those reading this book and contacting me with their personal experience. You may have witnessed a warning from God in another way than a dream. It could have come through a vision, that gut feeling, simple intuition, an angelic visitation, a sign, or simply waking up in the middle of the night and sensing something is terribly wrong. In any case, I would ask that you take the time and email it to me at The Interpreter's email address: Info@TheInterpretersView.com. I would ask that the story would be yours or in the words of the one who received the actual warning.

I believe there will be so many testimonies of this act of God that the evidence of these real stories will be irrefutable. They will strengthen our faith and the faith of the skeptics. They will help save lives. It is my sincere hope that this book has been a wake up call. It is my hope that if and when we receive a warning dream from God in the future, we will be able to respond and cancel that assignment. Even if it is or not a literal warning, I hope we will take my advice and err on the side of caution and take the dream to God in prayer.

My main objective of this book is to make people aware of the undeniable evidence. There *is* a force in the universe outside of us that, out of love, gives warning of the powers of darkness that come to bring destruction in our lives. I would encourage those who are not Christians to find out the method in which you can counter such an attack according to your belief system. If it is found that there is no means in that belief system that provides the dreamer the authority to put this foe down, I would invite you to call upon God through Jesus Christ who has the power to overcome these powers of darkness that exist. But, in any case, please do cry out to the Giver of these dreams. As we learn to sleep with our eyes open, I am confident we can make a difference. Instead of being victims of tragedies in life, we can become overcoming victors and can truly have life, and life more abundantly.

ABOUT THE AUTHOR

Craig has interpreted over 5,000 dreams in the past eight years and operates in a prophetic/teacher gifting, testifying the manifold ways God is speaking to us on the earth. He gives powerful testimony to his and others experiences through dreams, visions, and other revelatory encounters.

Under the name of "The Interpreters" Craig teaches Dream Classes, Workshops , "Hearing God Classes". He has facilitated "Hearing Group Meetings" for those wanting to continue growing in the area hearing God's voice and dream interpretation. He has recently expanded his ministry in the area of various Kingdom of God teachings and book writing.

Craig has been serving the Lord for 36 years and currently lives in St. Cloud, Minnesota with his wife Vicky, who accompanies him on most ministry occasions. They have three grown children.

You can contact Craig at:
Craig Groethe
c/o The Interpreters
801 13th Avenue South
St. Cloud, MN 56301
Phone: 320-255-1202
E-mail: craig@TheInterpretersView.com

Share your personal warning dreams and
stories at: TheInterpretersView.com

VISIT US ONLINE

Join Our Mailing List
Buy Books
Share Your Story

TheInterpretersView.com

or write: Info@TheInterpretersView.com
The Interpreters | 801 13th Avenue South | St. Cloud, MN 56301